Sailing with Vancouver

Sailing with Vancouver

A modern sea dog, antique charts
and a voyage through time

SAM MCKINNEY

TOUCHWOOD
EDITIONS

The information in this book is true and complete to the best of
the author's knowledge. All recommendations are made without
guarantee on the part of the author or the publisher.

Cover and interior design by Colin Parks
Edited by Marlyn Horsdal
Cover photo by HowardOates, istockphoto.com

Maps: George Vancouver map page ix courtesy of Oregon
Historical Society; maps pages x to xiii by Les Hopkins.

We acknowledge the financial support of the Government of
Canada through the Canada Book Fund and the Province of
British Columbia through the Book Publishing Tax Credit.

NATIONAL LIBRARY OF CANADA CATALOGUING IN PUBLICATION DATA

McKinney, Sam, 1927-, author
Sailing with Vancouver : a modern sea dog, antique charts and a voyage
through time / Sam McKinney. — Updated edition.

Includes bibliographical references.
Issued in print and electronic formats.
ISBN 978-1-77151-264-0 (softcover).

1. McKinney, Sam, 1927- —Travel—Northwest Coast of North America.
2. Vancouver, George, 1757-1798. 3. Sailing—Northwest Coast of North America.
4. Northwest Coast of North America—Discovery and exploration—British.
5. Northwest Coast of North America—Description and travel. I. Title.

GV776.15.B7M55   2018 910.9164'3   c2018-901408-3   c2018-901409-1

Canadä

PRINTED IN CANADA AT FRIESENS

22 21 20 19 18   1 2 3 4 5

Acknowledgments

TO WRITE A BOOK IS TO INDEBT THE AUTHOR TO MANY, AND IT IS a debt I fully acknowledge. Some, I can personally thank. John Weir, of course, for building *Kea* and passing it to me, along with its superior craftsmanship and tradition.

The book is largely drawn from the three volumes of W. Kaye Lamb's *George Vancouver, A Voyage of Discovery to the North Pacific*, loaned to me by my friend Jim Delgado, director of the Vancouver Maritime Museum. For other quoted material, I have to confess that I am an inveterate clipper and copier of bits of text that appeal to me; I put them in my "Miscellaneous" file without noting page numbers and the like, and I apologize for the incomplete attributions. The titles are in the bibliography, and I hope this at least indicates my great appreciation of the authors.

The maps were drawn by Portland designer Les Hopkins.

Contents

Maps

George Vancouver's great chart, drawn in 1792, of Puget Sound,
the Strait of Georgia, and Queen Charlotte Strait.

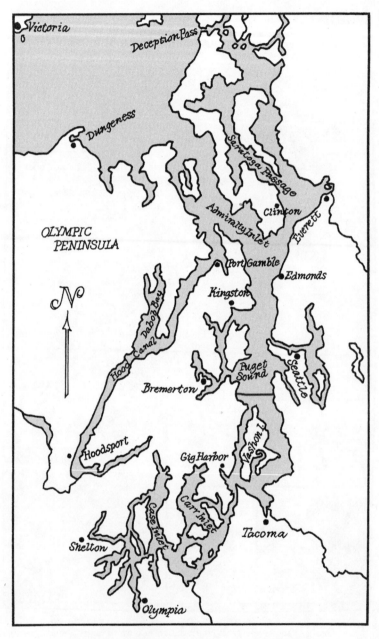

Puget Sound, explored by Peter Puget in 1792, is *Kea*'s home.

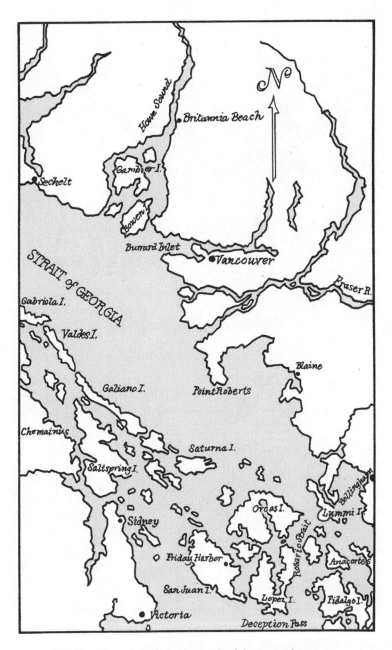

The San Juan and Gulf islands: jewels of the Strait of Georgia.

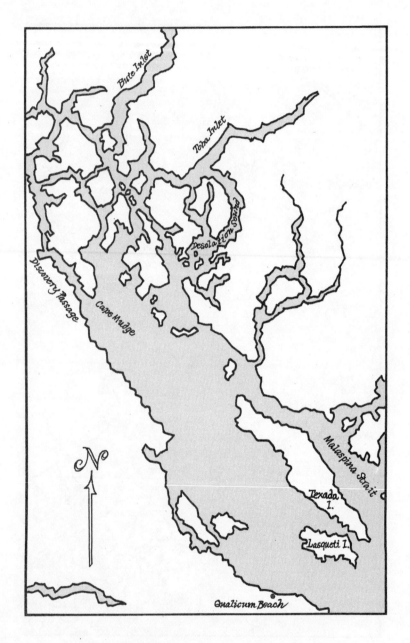

James Johnstone travelled through this labyrinth
to find his way to the Pacific.

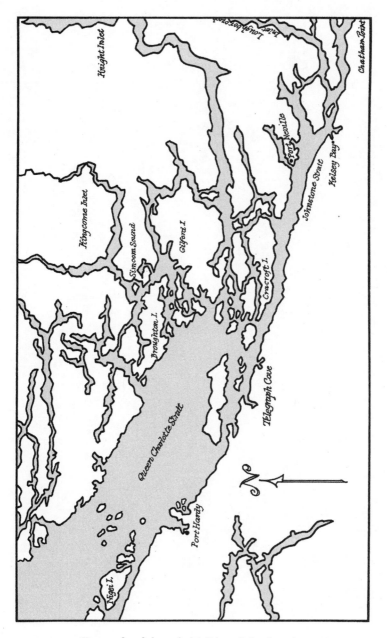

Kea wandered through this Eden of islands in the
Broughton Archipelago.

I.

Rendezvous with History

DOWN IN THE DEEP HOLLOWS BETWEEN THE HUGE SWELLS, I COULD see nothing. Nothing except the silent advance of the next mounded crest. Then, as the front slope of the wave slid under me and lifted the boat, I could get a short glimpse of the black line of the north-west coast to the east. Then, down in a hollow again and nothing around me but the sea.

The swells, with nothing to impede them, rolled eastward toward the shore, grey-green and silent, to break at the foot of Cape Flattery, that 1,500-foot-high prow of land that forms the far north-western point of Washington. The air was damp, smelling strongly of salt and seaweed: old smells, smells of the sea and time itself. Gulls dropped through a ceiling of mist, fluttered their wings, and settled in the wake of my boat. White specks of seabirds floating on the swells fluttered up in front of me and then settled again in clusters to preen themselves and swim about in tiny circles. My small sailboat and I were barely a shadow on the empty sea as we rolled there, encircled by the watery ring that surrounded us. Time was reduced to the simple rhythm of one passing wave, followed by another, and another.

Had I been in this location off the cape on the morning of April 28, 1792, I would have watched the slow arrival of two sailing ships, running north along the coast before the wind on a course that would carry them in from the sea toward the cape and into the opening of the Strait of Juan de Fuca.

The lead ship was the HMS *Discovery*, commanded by 34-year-old George Vancouver. The second ship was the HMS *Chatham*, commanded by 30-year-old William Broughton. Tired and sea weary were these men and their ships, after a 13-month voyage out from England, around the Cape of Good Hope to the Hawaiian Islands. From Hawaii, they sailed north to Cape Flattery where they entered the Strait of Juan de Fuca.

I had gone offshore in my boat to fall in behind the wakes of these two ships as they entered the strait and then to follow their voyages of exploration through the Inland Sea of Puget Sound, the Strait of Georgia and Queen Charlotte Strait. With the journal Vancouver wrote of this expedition and the chart he drew in my possession, I turned in from the sea to follow the two ships.

Myth, legend and fog ... these were blankets of ignorance hovering over the northwest coast in the centuries after Columbus's voyage to the New World. It was a far corner of the world, so remote that the novelist Jonathan Swift could, in 1726, place there the fantasy land of Brobdingnag, discovered by Gulliver in his travels.

Though unseen by Europeans, the northwest coast was claimed by Spain because of the treaty it had signed with Portugal in 1494 giving Spain colonizing rights to all lands west of a line drawn down the western Atlantic. When Spanish explorer Vasco Nunez de Balboa crossed the Isthmus of Panama in 1513 to the Pacific Ocean, he added its shores to the Spanish claim, and Spain began its colonizing of the Pacific coasts of South and Central America, Mexico and Lower California.

Then, in 1725, Peter the Great of Russia asked a simple question: Is the far northeastern coast of Asia linked to North America or are the two continents separated by water? Vitus Bering, a Dane, was sent out to answer this question. On his first voyage he sailed through the strait bearing his name that separates the two continents. On his second voyage in 1741 he reached the coast of southern Alaska.

These incursions into what Spain considered its Hispanic waters prompted a number of Spanish exploring voyages north along the Pacific Coast. Juan Perez in 1774 reached the Queen Charlotte Islands. Juan Francisco de la Bodega y Quadra in 1775 reached Sitka Sound. For all the enterprise of these Spanish voyages, they yielded little information about the northwest coast, and what knowledge was gained was largely held in secret by Spain.

James Cook, on his third and last great exploration from 1776 to 1778 in the ships *Resolution* and *Discovery,* brought the outline of the northwest coast into the orbit of geographical knowledge. The dual mission of this voyage was to search for a possible Pacific connection to a Northwest Passage that would give England a trading route to the Orient and to establish a British claim to the coast north of the 45th parallel.

Cook sighted the Oregon coast in March 1778, sailed north, missed the entry to the Strait of Juan de Fuca, and came to anchor in Nootka Sound on the west coast of Vancouver Island. He then sailed north along the Alaskan shore, through the Aleutian Islands chain and Bering Strait and into the Arctic Ocean, where ice blocked his way. After that, he sailed to Hawaii, where he was killed by natives.

What separated Cook's second voyage, 1772 to 1775, and his last voyage from all other previous maritime voyages was his ability to accurately determine his longitude by using a newly invented clock capable of maintaining accurate time at sea. On the basis of the time difference between England's Greenwich time and Cook's shipboard time, his longitude — a measure of time — could be determined east or west from Greenwich. Another improvement introduced by Cook was the elimination of the dreaded disease scurvy by insisting on serving his crew such antiscorbutics as pickled cabbage, spruce beer, fresh fruits and vegetables whenever possible. Watching and learning on Cook's second and third voyages was the young midshipman George Vancouver, later to be given his own expedition to follow up and complete the charting of the northwest coast begun by his mentor, James Cook.

George Vancouver was born in 1758 in the Norfolk town of King's Lynn on the east coast of England. At 14 he began his naval career as a midshipman on Cook's second voyage. The mission of this voyage was to search the southern oceans for Terra Australis Incognito, the southern continent geographers believed existed to counterbalance the continents of the northern hemisphere.

Returning to England, Vancouver was promoted to lieutenant, and for the next few years he saw active service under Commodore Alan Gardner in the West Indies, where he was given the job of surveying and charting the Jamaican ports of Port Royal and Kingston Harbour. The results impressed Gardner and led to Vancouver's being promoted to the rank of commodore in command of an expedition to the northwest coast with two ships, the *Discovery* and the *Chatham*.

In the years between the Cook and Vancouver voyages, Spain sent Esteban Martinez to Nootka Sound to build a fort in an effort to assert its claim to the northwest coast. An English ship, the *Argonaut,* entered the sound and was seized by Martinez. When news of this incident reached London, John Meares — the owner of the ship — released an inflammatory account of the incident. The affair was seen by England as an affront to the freedom of Pacific navigation, and England and Spain were brought to the verge of war. The Nootka Convention settled the squabble, but its terms were vague, with many details unresolved. The first objective of Vancouver's voyage to the northwest coast was to negotiate treaty terms that would be acceptable to both Great Britain and Spain.

His second objective was to complete the coastal survey begun by Cook. The third objective, spelled out in the written instructions he received from the British admiralty, ordered him to secure "accurate information with respect to the nature and extent of any water-communication which may tend, in any considerable degree, to facilitate intercourse, for the purposes of commerce, between the north-west coast, and the country upon the opposite side of the continent, which are inhabited or occupied by His Majesty's subjects."

In plain language, Vancouver was ordered to search for a Pacific opening to a water passage over the top of the North American continent. This Northwest Passage, as it was called, does not exist, but as was the case with El Dorado, Shangri-La and Utopia, that did not prevent desire and imagination from believing it did. As a theme, as something to "discover," the search for the Northwest Passage illustrates the continuity of the great period of maritime exploration that began with the Columbus voyage of 1492 to find a sea route to the Orient. Vancouver would continue the search, and one of his great contributions to maritime exploration was to find that such a passage — as a viable commercial waterway north of North America — did not exist.

The expedition consisted of two ships and 184 men. The *Discovery*, with a complement of 162 men, was 99 feet long, drew 15 feet, 6 inches, and weighed 330 tons. By all accounts, the ship was well suited for the voyage.

The smaller *Chatham*, 131 tons and 53 feet long, had a complement of 76 men. The *Chatham's* master, James Johnstone, found his ship a poor sailer, unstable and slow. In his journal, Johnstone described the vessel as "the most improper Vessel that could have been pitched upon ... & for sailing we have not been a match for the Dullest Merchant Vessel we have met with."

Officers on the two ships, in addition to Vancouver, were as follows:

Aboard the *Discovery:*

> Zachary Mudge, first lieutenant, age 22;
> Peter Puget, second lieutenant, age unknown;
> Joseph Baker, third lieutenant, age unknown;
> Joseph Whidbey, master, age unknown.

Aboard the *Chatham:*

> William Broughton, captain, age 30;
> James Johnstone, master, age 23.

To honour their contributions to the voyage, the names of each of these officers would be left behind on the chart Vancouver drew of the coast — names that remain there today.

Below decks, the two ships carried an astonishing cargo of trade items that included axes, hatchets, adzes, chisels, hammers, nails, saws, pocket knives, bar iron, brass and copper sheets, needles, scarlet cloth, feathers and coloured beads.

The two ships sailed from Falmouth on April 1, 1791. The year-long voyage to the northwest coast took them around the Cape of Good Hope, along the southern coast of Australia, and to Tahiti and the Hawaiian Islands. On April 18, 1792, the two ships reached North America in the area of Mendocino, California, where Vancouver began his coastal charting. Sailing northward along the coast, he failed to realize that a small bay he passed was the mouth of the Columbia River.

Until the ships rounded Cape Flattery and entered the Strait of Juan de Fuca, Vancouver's voyage had essentially followed the route he had taken with Cook in 1778. Vancouver, as he sailed into the strait, departed from Cook's shadow and began the voyage of exploration that would give him his prominent role in the history of maritime exploration.

In my little boat, I tagged along, 200-odd years later.

II.

Two Voyages of Discovery

IF WE ARE TO TRAVEL TOGETHER IN THIS BOOK THROUGH THE Inland Sea, following in the wake of Vancouver, introductions are in order: an introduction of myself and my reasons for wanting to retrace the Vancouver voyage.

My friend Bill Garden, the distinguished northwest marine architect, describes modern boating "as a high-speed run from one marina to another on a tide of affluence." I wanted a different kind of boating, something with a purpose and a discipline, something that would also relate to my interest in 18th-century maritime exploration and give me a historical perspective on what I call the Inland Sea. The retracing of the Vancouver expedition offered the fulfilment of both ambitions.

His voyage of more than two centuries ago recorded some of the first encounters between the original tribal people of the

Inland Sea and Europeans. He named many of the places found on today's charts of these waters, and the origins of these names are an important part of their history. Vancouver spent less than five months exploring and charting these intricate waters. I spent a spring and a summer retracing that route, discovering along the way the contrasts between how this Inland Sea and its surrounding shores looked over two centuries ago and how it appears today. It is, of course, a much-altered seascape of cities, small towns, industries, commercial developments and residential shorelines. But much of what I saw remains largely as Vancouver and his men would have seen it, and many times I could say to myself: That island, that cove, that forested slope, is exactly what Vancouver and his men would have seen more than 200 years ago.

For me, an avid sailor, my own voyage in the track of the Vancouver expedition was a challenging adventure. In my boat, I encountered the same seas, tides, winds and weather that those explorers confronted. These conditions are ever the same and in encountering them — even though my boat was equipped with an engine and modern electronics — I shared with Vancouver and his men the link of vulnerability that is the ever-present condition of all people who go to sea: fear, boredom and fatigue.

Even so, my relative comfort and security was in sharp contrast to those men in wooden sailing ships and open boats who travelled this uncharted sea of unknown depths, distances, tides, currents, winds and reefs. What, I wondered, were their emotions in the immensity of this great unknown? Their fears? Their sense of time and distance? They ate coarse food, spent long hours rowing and sailing in open boats, camped — wet and cold — on rocky shores, encountered natives of foreign and potentially threatening dispositions. In spite of these adversities, however, and by diligence and determination, they were able to draw a chart of a coastline that was so accurate it was used well into the 20th century. Then, imagining the hardships, the courage and the dedication of these men, I had to ask these questions:

What kind of men were they who, with so little, accomplished so much? What god, luck, destiny or duty was it that lay behind their indomitable will, perseverance and endurance? For many, of course, it was merely a job to be done, and failure brought the threat of the lash; no romantic, adventurous voyage was this expedition for such men, so how, I wondered, were they able to survive, in both mind and body, the hardships they endured?

And this I asked of myself: Could I have been one of them? To this question, I have no answer, because nothing in my voyage came even close to duplicating any of the conditions endured by the men of the Vancouver expedition. The other question I asked of myself was this: Would I have liked to have been a member of the expedition and, if so, why?

To this question, I give an unqualified yes. The answer to why is because of who I am: a restless person, who has always been on the move toward the edge of what he knows, with the desire to cross over that edge to something unknown where the outcome is in doubt. It is only along the journey toward that edge that I feel alive, no longer a passive spectator of life but a participant at the threshold of something that gives significance to the present moment and a passionate anticipation for the unknown future. That, I think, is the outlook or personality of the explorer, so as an explorer of past and present, I followed in the wake of Vancouver through the Inland Sea.

Compensating for the difficulties of rain, wind and fatigue that I encountered on my own voyage was the pleasurable historical detective work I dealt with in connecting journal entries to the routes taken by Vancouver and his men through these waters. This research gave my cruise an established course of historical significance to follow rather than it being a wandering pleasure voyage of no particular route, destination or purpose. The familiar geography of a well-known harbour or cape was given a historical dimension by knowing something of what happened there, how it was seen in another century, and the reason for the name it was given. In this way, I, too, travelled as an explorer, believing that exploration lies not so much in what is seen but in *how* it is seen. Within that perspective, I discovered along my way messages written for everyone in rock, wave, wind, tide and history.

To follow Vancouver's track, I had a collection of more than 20 charts covering the waters he explored. But for tracing his actual voyage, I had a photographic copy of the single chart he drew of the area of those 20 charts. Titled "A Chart showing part of the Coast of N.W. America with the tracks of His Majesty's Sloop Discovery and Armed Tender Chatham," it is an exquisite piece of draftsmanship. Its accuracy in defining channels, inlets, headlands and capes is such that I could have thrown out the 20 modern charts I carried and navigated solely with the Vancouver chart and his journal.

III.

A Man and His Boat

HAVING EXPLAINED THE "WHY" OF MY VOYAGE, I NOW INVITE YOU
to step aboard my boat, *Kea*, and I will tell you the story of both of
us. Pour yourself a cup of tea or a glass of rum, then let your eyes
wander around the inside cabin of this 25-foot wooden boat. See
how the light from the swinging kerosene lantern is reflected in
the varnished mahogany of the cabin sides, curved roof beams and
cupboard doors and in the soft glow of brass portholes. Around us,
books on tide, navigation, maritime history and ocean voyages line
the shelves over each bunk. Tucked away in crannies and drawers
are heavy woollen sweaters, socks and gloves. By the companion-
way hangs rain gear, parkas, pants and wide-brimmed foul-weather
hats. In the narrow recess of the fo'c's'le, bagged sails and coils of
rope are hung from hooks. Ask me, and I can tell you what lies
behind every closed cupboard and drawer: tools, sewing kits, spare

blocks, bright shackles, binoculars, a brass foghorn, protractors, dividers and charts. You can tell by what's around us that the boat and I are a matched pair, both of us on the downhill side of our prime and leaning toward the traditional way of things: caulked wooden planks, pine tar, diesel oil, woollen underwear, pipe smoke and Navy rum.

I bought this boat as a present to myself on my 70th birthday, bought it because I needed to break out from under a cloud of uselessness and boredom that hung over me. Such feelings, I found, came naturally with old age, along with the disgust I felt for the skinny, withered torso I would see in the mirror as I stepped from the shower, the fumbling for the wrong key at the front door and the lost hats, gloves and umbrellas I left behind in restaurants and stores. What were my alternatives? I could have joined an exercise class and fought back stiffness. Tied a string to my gloves. Grown a beard to hide the wrinkles. Call the cane a walking stick. Move to that retirement home in a place of sun that would be gated, guarded and gardened. A new career? Impossible. A hobby? How boring. I could have bought a new wardrobe, changed my image from drab sparrow-grey tweeds to something colourful and sporty to go along with the purchase of a red convertible car, one of those flashy imported models. But I am content with my one well-worn old wool jacket and I am determined to get 500,000 miles out of my old Volvo.

Around the house, I was only in her way. I cleaned the cat box, took out the garbage, lifted my feet when she vacuumed the rug and patiently pushed the cart behind her in the grocery store. And yet I led a good life: adored wife of 30 years, comfortable home, reasonable health and financial security. Why, then, that disease of longing for something else when, by all accounts, I should have been content with what I had? The answer was simple: because of who I am and how the person within me likes to live. So I began looking for a sailboat.

Depressing was the search — plastic look-alikes, designed for factory production in cookie-cutter shapes, to my eye indistinguishable from each other and at prices far beyond my reach. What I was looking for was a stout little wooden sailboat, but when I asked the young khaki- and tennis-shoe-clad marina salesmen about a wooden boat, they looked at me with a dismissive gaze. "Not many of those around anymore, Dad," they reminded me.

Success in my search came from a lucky coincidence, one of those intersections of events that I believe determine many aspects of life: man meets woman and two lives are changed; right place at the right time and a new career begins. This particular intersection came because of a book I had read, followed by an ad I found in a boating magazine. The book, *My Old Man and the Sea*, told the story of a voyage around Cape Horn by the father-and-son team of David and Daniel Hays. I found the story fascinating, but what impressed me most was that they had made this voyage in a boat of the Vertue class, designed in 1938 by the famous English marine architect Laurent Giles. Many of these boats have made remarkable voyages, including the one named *Sparrow*, which the Hays sailed on their 17,000-mile voyage around the Horn.

I finished the book, marvelled at the father-son adventures, but remembered the story mostly because of what they had accomplished in that little sloop. A few weeks later, I came across a small ad in the October 2002 issue of *WoodenBoat*. It read: "25' Vertue No. 142. One owner," followed by a telephone number for a man named John Weir in Nanaimo, B.C. Hesitantly, almost fearfully, I laid down the magazine, took a few deep breaths, then dialled the number. As I waited for an answer, thoughts sped through my mind: "This is ridiculous. Hang up now before it's too late, before you commit yourself to something you are too old to do and can't afford anyhow." But another voice said, "You must try, otherwise ..." and John Weir answered the phone.

"Yes," he said in response to my question, "I have my Vertue for sail, built it myself in 1968." Over the phone, he described it to me. Sight unseen, I knew I wanted to buy his boat, provided it passed a survey. He agreed to arrange for the survey, usually paid for by the prospective buyer.

"Shall I send you a cheque for the haul-out and survey?" I asked.

"No," replied John, in his very soft but pronounced English accent. "I'll send you the results of the survey, you come look at the boat, and we'll sort it out then."

"John," I confessed, "I'm old-fashioned. A man's word and a handshake is what I trust. Can we work together on that basis?"

"There's no other way as far as I'm concerned," he replied.

I had one last question: "John, why are you selling the boat?"

"Because," he answered, "I'll soon be 70 years old."

I hesitated a moment, then said, "John, the reason I would be buying your boat is because I *am* 70." On that, we both laughed and ended our conversation.

You can get married on a whim; 10 dollars for a licence, the exchange of a few words and you take unto yourself a wife and hope for the best. Not so when you buy a boat; it must be submitted to an intimate inspection of parts and pieces a bride would never permit. That inspection is called "the survey." It is performed by a licensed professional surveyor who represents neither buyer nor seller in his appraisal of a boat's price, condition and equipment. It is his job to poke and peer into the inner recesses, stick an ice pick into frames and planking, probing for rot, and look for faulty wiring and worn places in rigging and sails. Both John and I anxiously awaited the surveyor's diagnosis and comments, hoping for a favourable report: John because he wanted to sell the boat, me because I wanted to buy it. The surveyor held our mutual desires in the outcome of his clinical examination of this modest, proud little boat hauled out of the water and sitting on the ways, naked and violated in the most intimate ways.

When the survey was completed, John sent me a copy along with a few pictures. The pictures showed a trim little sloop with traditional red tanbark sails. The survey described the dimensions of the boat: Overall length, 25 feet; beam, 7 feet; draft, 4 feet, 6 inches; displacement, 11,000 pounds including 4,000 pounds of outside lead ballast. Construction of the boat was described as carvel planked, bronze fastened to bent oak frames. Stays and shrouds of the standing rigging were made of quarter-inch stainless-steel wire connected to bronze turnbuckles and stainless-steel chainplates bolted to inside frames. The sail inventory was extensive: main, two jibs, a storm trysail and a spinnaker.

Ground tackle consisted of two anchors on stem rollers with 200 feet of quarter-inch chain. The boat was also equipped with wind-vane steering and a 10-horsepower Yanmar diesel engine. Decks and cabin trunk were built of teak. The surveyor found no rot in either planks or frames and commented on the unusually fine workmanship throughout the boat.

I called John and told him that, based on the survey, I would buy his boat. "Better come up and look at it first," he advised. "Then you can decide." I agreed to his sensible advice and we set a date for me to fly up to Nanaimo on Vancouver Island to look at the boat that, in my mind, I had already bought.

What was amazing about that decision was the immediate effect it had on my life. Suddenly, it was as though my thoughts for the future were contained within a colourful bubble, iridescent in its mingling of dreams, ambitions, hopes and desires. It followed me like a balloon in my reveries, awakened me to days of quiet anticipation and blurred the line between dreams of the day and the night. Northwest author Don Berry describes something of this condition in his book *To Build a Ship:*

> At first it was like the beginning of a love affair. We tended to go around grinning foolishly at each other ... because we shared a secret that nobody else could touch. We were going to build a Ship ... For the first time I understood things the history books left out ... the feeling a man suddenly gets in his belly that he can change the way things are. With the strength of his back and arms and brain, he can make things different ... For the first time he realizes there is more to living than merely submitting.

Anticipating the purchase of this boat, I had those feelings described by Don Berry. I accepted that I could not do anything about my advanced age but with a boat to sail, I had the liberating feeling that I did not have to totally submit to the years. Beowulf, the eighth-century English warrior, gave me a mark to reach for with this advice:

> Harder should be the spirit
> The heart all the bolder

Greater the courage
As the strength grows less.

John Weir, short, stocky and fully bearded, met me at the Nanaimo airport and drove us to the marina at Boat Harbour where the boat was moored. I carried with me a certified cheque for the agreed price of the boat that I wanted to hand over to John as soon as I stepped aboard.

"Wait," he said, "till you see how it sails, then decide whether or not to buy it."

I think that in slowing my eagerness to hand him the cheque for the boat, he was really looking me over to see if he approved of me as the new owner of the boat his very skilful hands had built, that he had sailed throughout Canadian waters, and that he obviously had loved and cared for very much. John had named the boat *Kea,* which, he explained, was a small New Zealand bird.

As a result of the sailing demonstration, I approved of the boat and John approved of me. When we returned to the dock, I handed him the cheque and I became *Kea*'s new owner.

Patiently, John then described to me the workings of the diesel engine, the kerosene stove and the simple electrical system. Little touches of his personality and his practical boat know-how were apparent in the way the halyards were organized, the fuel tanks fitted, spare parts and tools stored, the location of the bilge pumps and in many other details that had been worked out over the years he had sailed and lived aboard *Kea.* Looking around, I could clearly see that *Kea* did not need any repairs or new equipment. He sold it to me in a sail-away condition, complete with pots, pans, dishes, spare parts, extra coils of ropes and a box of tools.

The cheque I gave to John was enclosed in a book I had written. I signed my name on the flyleaf of the book along with a note that read: "Thanks John for a wonderful boat. I will take good care of your *Kea*." He stepped ashore, walked up the dock, turned for one last look at the boat, no longer his, and drove away.

I went below for a moment of privacy, touched the cabin sides, ran my hand along the smooth surface of the navigating table, stretched out on one of the bunks and looked up at the curving beams of the cabin roof. The last of the October light gave a soft glow to the mellowed colour of teak and mahogany panelling, the glint of brass portholes and the expressed strength of the mast, anchored in place by supporting knees and iron bands. "Happy birthday," I murmured to myself. "You have given yourself one hell of a fine boat as a birthday gift."

It was later that I read about the history and accomplishments of the Vertue class in a *WoodenBoat* magazine article by Andrew Pool entitled "Masterpiece: the Vertue and Her Achievements" (Volume 24, 1978). The article begins with a description of the boat: "By today's standards it is old fashioned with its heavy displacement, cutter rig, small cockpit, narrow beam ... but it has its virtues. It will run true as a dart, heave-to like an old duck, work its way to windward in relative comfort when the going gets tough, and sail itself beautifully — characteristics that few modern 25 footers can boast."

The boat first appeared on the English yachting scene prior to World War II and since then many have been built in boatyards around the world, most of them in England. It takes its name from a 750-mile cruise to the Bay of Biscay made by Lawrence Biddle in 1939. For that cruise, an English sailing club presented Biddle with its prestigious Vertue Cup and that cup gave the name to this particular class of boat.

The Vertue's fame spread after Humphrey Barton's 3,500-mile Atlantic crossing from England to New York in *Vertue XXXV*, so named because it was the 35th Vertue to be built. His boat survived a hurricane in that crossing. *Cardinal Vertue,* skippered by Dr. David Lewis, was an entry in the first single-handed Trans-Atlantic Race in 1960, competing with the famous racers Francis Chichester and H. G. "Blondie" Hasler. *Cardinal Vertue* was then sold and its new owner, Bill Nance, sailed it around the world. It was on the voyage from Australia to Cape Horn that Nance set the record (for then) for a long-distance passage of 122 miles a day over a period of 53 days. Since then, according to the *WoodenBoat* article, "long voyages completed by Vertues have become so commonplace that the records are incomplete." Pool concludes his article:

> All these voyages, not to mention many ambitious summer cruises, have been made by yachts of the same class, a boat with enormous aesthetic appeal, as much admired for her good looks as for her sea-keeping qualities, and [in a boat] which is only 25'3" long. It is a little ironic that such a small, fundamentally conservative, unprepossessing boat should become the hallmark of Laurent Giles and Partners, a firm which has produced stellar ocean racers and large luxury yachts whose innovations have influenced the whole course of yachting history. But perhaps there is a lesson in this, and a tribute to a designer who was willing to focus all of his creative energy on what could only have been seen at the time as a relatively minor design, in pursuit of excellence — the perfect expression of a simple concept. We can all tip our hats to his success, the handsome, able, tough and beloved Vertue. No vessel afloat can top her.

With a friend, I brought the boat back from Boat Harbor to its new home port in Boston Harbor at the southern end of Puget Sound. The following weekend, I packed all my boating gear into a bag and drove from my Portland home back to Boston Harbor. My project was to familiarize myself with the boat and its equipment, to inventory what John had stored away in its many drawers and cupboards. Also, by stowing my clothing and equipment aboard, I wanted to insert my personality into the boat, to make it "mine." John's personality, his way of doing things, permeated the boat in the physical evidence of the tools and equipment he had accumulated over the 30 years or so that he had sailed it.

This, I sorted out and reorganized to suit my comfort and convenience. What would remain of John were his little tricks of woodworking genius that gave to the boat the charm and beauty of a handcrafted work of art: the clean-line planking, fastened with bronze rivets to the steam-bent frames; the precise lines of the teak planks contouring the gentle curve of the deck; the moulded corner pieces of the cockpit well; the strong mahogany cabin sides; the little wooden buttons that prevented drawers from opening; the brass-hinged top of the navigating table; the cross-over drains of the cockpit and the grab rails running along the top of the coach roof and the full length of the cabin interior. And there were more surprises as I opened drawers, bins, boxes and cupboards: a complete tool kit; extra diaphragms for the two pumps; pots, pans and dishes; coils of extra rope; a safety harness for working on deck; a kerosene anchor riding light; a sounding lead and four headsails neatly stowed in sail bags. In his two-page list of instructions on how to do things, John left a note saying that before handing the boat over to me, he had filled the water and fuel tanks and the kerosene tank for the galley stove, and changed the oils and the engine filter. There was nothing for me to repair or paint or remodel. To make it mine,

I just wallowed in the satisfaction that the boat, all of its parts and pieces, its ropes, sails and equipment, now belonged to me, not so much as a possession but as the heritage of a legendary designer and a master craftsman, a legacy for me to respect in the way I cared for and sailed the boat.

And now that I have introduced to you myself and my boat, I can sail up the Strait of Juan de Fuca, driven by the same winds and tide that drove Vancouver's ships in from the Pacific to begin the exploration of the Inland Sea.

IV.

Mediterranean of the North

GEORGE VANCOUVER WROTE THIS AS HIS SHIP, HMS *DISCOVERY*, approached the Strait of Juan de Fuca in April of 1792: "Our curiosity was much excited to explore the promised expansive Mediterranean ocean which by various accounts is said to have existence in these waters."

A "Mediterranean ocean." I like that term as a description of the waters of the Strait of Juan de Fuca, Puget Sound, the Strait of Georgia and Queen Charlotte Strait. It groups together all the separately named waters of the United States and southern British Columbia into a single body of water. One sea, a Mediterranean of the North that I take the liberty of calling the Inland Sea.

But different from that sea of antiquity is this Mediterranean of the North. It is a mountain-ringed sea, carved by rivers of ice that left in their retreat a labyrinth of channels, inlets, fjords and island mazes that lies like the dissembled pieces of a huge jigsaw pattern. In some places, sea and shore are exposed to the full force of winds blowing in from the Pacific. In other places, water passages are scoured by tidal currents that form rapids, tumbling over falls of thundering water and whirlpools with sucking vortexes of swirling water.

And overall the sky is often a misty grey, sometimes wind-rent and sometimes of a clean, blue clarity that makes islands stand out like pieces of uncut jade, sea channels like ribbons of silver and forests that cloak the shoreline slopes like rumpled blankets of green.

It is a place of time: Geological time expressed in the glacial scouring of mountains and the weathering of rocks and cliffs by wind and tide. It is a place of life: life that swims in the sea, clings to rocks, burrows in mud and lofts on wings in the air. And it is a place of people: People who have lived on the shores of this sea for thousands of years and people who, over the last two centuries, have explored and settled along the shores of this two-nation Inland Sea. All of this — all time, all life — is shaped by the rhythms of this sea, the ebb and flow of the tides, and the passing moods of rain and wind and snow.

It is difficult to visualize today, but all of this was at one time covered by ice thousands of feet deep. Everywhere ice, rivers of ice that gave shape and depth to the Inland Sea as they carved and ground their way to the ocean. A huge arm of ice carved out the canyon of the Strait of Juan de Fuca that is over a thousand feet deep. Individual boulders carried by this mega-glacier were left at the 4,500-foot level on the northern and eastern slopes of the Olympic Mountains to the south of the strait.

The northern opening of the Inland Sea lies in Queen Charlotte Strait, between Cape Scott at the northern tip of Vancouver Island

and Cape Caution on the British Columbia mainland. The southern end is Budd Inlet in the lower end of Puget Sound. The straight-line distance from north to south is approximately 500 miles but that dimension is the lesser measurement of the Inland Sea. Its true size is defined by the thousand-mile, ragged, broken shoreline that encloses it. From the Strait of Juan de Fuca, this shoreline runs east to Port Townsend, then south to trace out the finger-like inlets of lower Puget Sound. Turning northward, the shoreline passes the cities of Seattle, Bellingham and Vancouver. From there, it turns northwestward to wander in and out of deep coastal fjords and through a hundred-mile-long island maze. Twisting and turning along its length, like the dribbled edge of spattered paint, the line concludes at Cape Scott and Cape Caution, to define the edge of one of the world's most complex and intricate inland seas.

For thousands of years, the shores and islands of the Inland Sea were home to the unique cultures of the northwest-coast Aboriginal peoples. For those thousands of years, they lived and flourished in their coastal villages, the hunter-gathers of a generous land and a rich sea that they exploited with an elaborate technology of wood, stone and bone. Their material objects — the canoes and paddles, totem poles, implements for eating — were elaborately carved in shapes and designs reflecting their beliefs in human and animal spirits. It was a culture that 2,500 years ago reached its full development in tradition, ritual and technology and then changed very little because it existed in near-perfect accord with the natural world of the sea and the forest that sustained it.

Imagine, a silence of millennia, broken only by the sound of the waves, the wind in the trees, the cry of the loon, the splash of the leaping salmon and the low murmur of tribal voices. Silence along these shores while Alexander the Great's army swept across Persia, Christian martyrs screamed as they were clawed by lions in the

Coliseum of Rome, Viking raiders landed on the British coast, and Columbus set out to discover the New World, a voyage that would culminate 300 years later with the first contact between these people of the Inland Sea and the world that lay beyond them.

In the span of a few years, they acquired things that changed their lives: A metal axe replaced a stone hatchet, and with it a tree could be felled in a day; a copper cooking kettle replaced the need to heat stones and drop them into a woven basket to boil a fish; a needle of steel replaced a bone awl; a sharp-edged metal knife replaced stone cutting tools; beads of glass replaced shells and feathers for decorative use and the gun — oh yes, the gun — replaced the bow and the spear.

The exchange rate for these wonders was not much at first: a few furs, some salmon. But the true costs were hidden and the real price was much greater. In the bottom of that Pandora's box of wonderful gifts was rum, which destroyed lives, and in its dark corners, the unseen virus that caused devastating epidemics of smallpox.

When travelling this sea in my boat, I often thought about these noble people, some still living but many gone. It was more than regret that I felt at their passing. It was as though something of the essential soul of the Inland Sea had disappeared with their passing, along with their art and beliefs that expressed the moods and mystery of water, land, sky, forest, fish and animal.

The words of Barry Lopez, written in one of the final essays in his book *Arctic Dreams*, are copied on the front page of the journal I kept as I travelled. They were helpful words because they reminded me that I was not alone in my regret for the loss of things that can never again be. Wrote Lopez:

> No culture has yet solved the dilemma each has faced
> with the growth of a conscious mind: how to live a

moral and compassionate existence when one is fully aware of the blood, the horror inherent in all life, when one finds darkness not only in one's own culture but within oneself. If there is a stage at which an individual life becomes truly adult, it must be when one grasps the irony in its unfolding and accepts responsibility for a life lived in the midst of such a paradox. One must live in the middle of contradiction because if all contradictions were eliminated at once life would collapse. There are simply no answers to some of the great pressing questions. You continue to live them out, making your life a worthy expression of a leaning into the light.

And leaning into the light, I sailed on, following the two ships that would lead me through the still-magnificent waters of the Inland Sea.

V.

The Strait of Juan de Fuca

JUST SOUTH OF CAPE FLATTERY, WHERE *KEA* AND I PICKED UP THE track of the Vancouver expedition, stands a rock with the name de Fuca's Pillar. As I sailed in from the sea and toward the cape, I scanned the shoreline through binoculars and spotted this particular rock. My pilot book describes it as "a rocky column 157 feet high and 60 feet in diameter, leaning slightly NW." That description is fairly close to the one given by the man who claimed to have seen it over 400 years ago.

He was the Greek mariner Apostolos Valerianos, who went by the Spanish name of Juan de Fuca. He claimed that in 1592 the viceroy of Mexico sent him on an exploring expedition north along the Pacific Coast. On that voyage, he said, he found "a broad inlet of Sea, between 47 and 48 degrees of Latitude ... and at the entrance of this strait ... there is a great Hedland or Island, with an exceeding high Pinacle or spired Rocke, like a pillar thereupon."

Historians consider de Fuca's claim a myth. But the story, over the next few centuries, was intriguing to geographers of the time because the reported strait might have been a western opening to a Northwest Passage across the top of North America. Captain Charles Barkley, a British fur trader, found the entrance to the Strait of Juan de Fuca in 1787 and, believing de Fuca's story, gave his name to the strait.

As James Cook sailed along the northwest coast on his third and last voyage, he thought the Strait of Juan de Fuca was only "a small opening that flattered us with hopes of finding a harbour. These hopes lessened as we drew nearer; and at last, we had some reason to think that the opening was closed by low land. On this account I called the point of land ... Cape Flattery but closer examination proved the hopes to be vain." Cook, unaware of the huge strait that lay to the east of the cape, continued sailing north searching for that Northwest Passage until he was stopped by the impenetrable ice in the Bering Sea. And so, with an English-named cape standing over me at the opening to a Spanish-named strait, I headed *Kea* in from the ocean and sailed beneath the protecting gaze of the lighthouse standing on Tatoosh Island at the southern entrance to the strait.

A "bright star" is what James Swan, a Washington pioneer settler and author of *The Northwest Coast*, called the Tatoosh Island light as he tried to enter the strait. "The wind being adverse," he wrote, "we were obliged to beat across the entrance for five days without gaining anything. But every night we were cheered by the light of Tatoosh Island ... shining like a bright star amid the primeval gloom."

I think that a lighthouse, like the one on Tatoosh Island, is the classical architectural form of the marine and coastal landscapes. The simple but gracefully utilitarian shape of a lighthouse tower — like that of a sparse, white New England church — is a self-evident statement of its purpose. In both the lighthouse and the church, form and function merge in a kind of spiritual significance: light where there is darkness, steadfastness and safety. A lighthouse, standing at the outermost tip of a cape or clinging to some sea-swept rock, also suggests a harsh isolation within a lonely but peaceful solitude. And in the secular professions, none in literature and legend exceed the virtues and the dependable duty of the lighthouse keeper. In the myth created about him, he is always old, wise in the way of the sea and its weather, undaunted by hardship and protective — with his life, if need be — of the light given to him to keep.

The Strait of Juan de Fuca I was sailing through is 80 miles long and 12 to 16 miles wide. The international boundary between the United States and Canada runs down the centre of the strait, Washington's Olympic Mountains to the south, the coast of Vancouver Island to the north. Today, like a broad sea-highway, a traffic-separation system defined by electronic navigation aids divides the strait into inbound and outbound ship channels. Tides, pushing through the strait, carry to the southern end of Puget Sound and to the northern end of the Strait of Georgia.

The strait is a place of ferocious winds. *Sailing Directions* for the British Columbia coast warns: "The weather of the strait is change-able and in few places of the world is the navigator required to be more cautious and vigilant than when entering it from the Pacific Ocean." To this was added the warning that winds above 50 knots are recorded in almost all months of the year.

I came into the strait on a strong westerly wind blowing 20 to 25 knots, stronger than any wind I had ever sailed with in *Kea*. Yet, I welcomed it as an opportunity to see if my practice hours of sailing had prepared me to handle the boat in such a wind.

When I first bought *Kea*, I had taught myself to sail it in the hard school of trial and error. My first attempts had been disasters of tangled rigging and sheets. I knew the location of each of the ropes and their purpose, but what I had trouble with was the sequential steps to be followed in getting up the sails. To get them right, I memorized the necessary steps and then played the game of captain and crew. The imagined captain would call out the orders to me, the crewman, with the name of "Dumbshit." The practice sessions went something like this:

"Okay, Dumbshit, first hook the halyards to the sails. Now head into the wind and take the stops off the mainsail, lift the boom out of its crutch and haul up the mainsail. Now go forward and lift the jib. Don't crawl, Dumbshit; get up and walk! Now get back to the cockpit, put the boat on course, adjust the main and jib sheets, slack the topping lift, tighten the boom vang and turn off the engine." If I did all that without making too many mistakes, the captain would let Dumbshit go below for a quick swig of rum.

After a few practice trips, I was able to sail without that demanding captain telling me what to do. But it wasn't easy for my somewhat stiff and not-too-agile 70-year-old body and I worried about how I would handle these tasks alone in a stiff wind. What particularly bothered me was the danger of falling overboard when I had to go forward to handle the various lines in lifting and dropping the sails. I knew that in sailing alone, a fall overboard would probably be fatal.

What I then did was to rig the boat so that solo-sailing would be easier and safer. I redirected all the lines that controlled the sails aft to where they could be handled in the safety and convenience of the cockpit. I also installed a self-furling jib system and rigged a line along both sides of the cabin trunk that I could tie myself to with a safety harness if I did have to go forward.

Re-rigging all the lines through new fairleads and cleats was the pleasant work of three or four weekends, interspersed with many trips to the marine supply store, much dockside advice by visitors and the occasional assistance of other boat owners. On the Sunday afternoon that I finished, I stood on the deck with the unattached main halyard in my hand, just checking the new system. Then, without thinking, I let go of the halyard for a second. In the wind, it swung out from the boat beyond my reach and went flying up to the top of the mast where it stuck in its sheave. New command for Dumbshit to memorize: "Don't ever let go of a halyard without first securing it to something."

What had to be done to retrieve the halyard was to go to the top of the mast in a bosun's chair and pull it back down. Forty feet up a mast and swinging in a bosun's chair, I thought, is not exactly a task suitable for an older man. I wanted a rigger or a small boy to do the job for the simple reason that I was rather afraid to go aloft myself.

Scotty is the friendly man at Boat Harbor always willing and able to give some damn fool person like myself a helping hand. "I'm too heavy to go aloft," he said as he observed my problem, "but I'll wind you up on your halyard winch."

Well, I figured that I shouldn't ask anyone to do something I was afraid of doing, so aloft I went and pulled the loose end of the halyard down as Scotty dropped me back to the safety of the deck. He dismissed my embarrassment for losing the halyard by stating, "A feller ain't a sailor until he has lost a halyard and gone aloft to capture it."

Now, running fast downwind through the Strait of Juan de Fuca, I felt both elation and fear as the boat lifted and dipped over the crests and troughs of the following waves. Elation because of the rush of the boat through the water; fear because I was not certain that I had full control of it and that an unintentional jibe might throw us broadside to wind and wave.

There is a feeling I have experienced when I am threatened by danger, a tightening of the stomach muscles that seems to grow outward from the solar plexus. When this happens, I try to calmly separate real danger from imagined danger. It is a trick I learned back in my mountaineering days. I called it assessing the *content* of the danger. How much of it was real, how much imagined through fear or unfamiliarity with the conditions or geography of the mountain? I applied my mountain trick to my wild, wind-driven sail up the Strait of Juan de Fuca and came up with this reassuring conclusion: Yes, the wind was strong, but it was nowhere near the winds encountered by Humphrey Barton as he sailed *Vertue XXXV* across the Atlantic, nor by the Hayses, father and son, who sailed their *Sparrow* around Cape Horn. *Kea,* therefore, was more than capable of dealing with this wind of the strait. The only danger was me and my apprehension of danger; I sat rigid at the tiller, over-steering as each wave passed beneath the boat and worried about what *could* happen rather than what *was* happening.

An hour passed, then another hour. My imagined dangers became the routine of sailing, with *Kea* simply doing what a sailboat that is well designed and built should do: yield to the wind, lift to the waves and stay its course. I ducked below to light my pipe and let the boat take command as we sailed up the strait in pursuit of two 18th-century sailing ships.

VI.

Cape Flattery and Foulweather Bluff

I SAILED IN ONLY A FRESH BREEZE UP THE STRAIT OF JUAN DE Fuca. The more typical weather of the strait — rain and a gale — carried the men of the *Discovery* and the *Chatham*. Weather, however, was the least difference between our two voyages. I had been at sea less than a day when I entered the strait, and I felt a great sense of relief as the green, forested shores enclosed me. I could only imagine the relief Vancouver and his men might have felt as they turned in from the open sea and approached these same shores. Behind them was a voyage of 393 days that had crossed three oceans. Behind them were long months of eating plain, monotonous food, days of cold, rain, storm and the merciless calms and heat of the tropics, all endured under the constant strain of impending danger as they lived, worked and slept in the constantly rolling and pitching ships. What they must have wanted was relief from these conditions, fresh water, and something even more urgent: land, solid earth to walk over. Eyes that had seen nothing for many days except the featureless expanse of an empty sea now eagerly looked up to hillsides mantled in a forest of green.

And there were other differences between our two voyages. I had charts with me that described the waters we were both about to enter. Charts that marked and named channels and passages, identified rock, reefs and shallow waters, showed the contours of shorelines and gave the locations of cities and town where I could buy supplies and converse with people of my own language and culture.

For the earlier expedition sailing up the strait, every mile travelled brought it farther into a void of the unknown. Questions and speculations, though probably unspoken, were no doubt troubling every man. Could safe passages be found? What were the prevailing winds? If the shores were peopled, would they be friendly or dangerous? For all its vast size and storms, the ocean they had just crossed had been the familiar world of these sailors, safe because they knew how to deal with its moods and dangers. Yes, there was relief in reaching land and protected waters, but also anxiety in not knowing what dangers might lie along those unknown shores.

But their mission was to make the unknown known and to carry out this objective, Captain Vancouver ordered Lieutenant William Broughton, commander of the smaller *Chatham*, to take the lead. Sail was shortened on both ships and men stood in the forward chains sounding the sea bottom with leads that touched nothing in the 400-foot depths of the strait just offshore.

Water, wood for cooking, the repair of sails and rigging and rest for the crew — the usual needs of ships and men after a long voyage — were uppermost in Vancouver's mind as the winds drove the two ships eastward through the strait. Friendly Makah Natives from Neah Bay urged Vancouver to stop at their village, but he considered the bay too exposed and sailed farther along the coast in search of a more protected anchorage. In rainy weather, about eight miles in from the entrance to the strait, the two ships anchored. This, the first anchorage of English ships in the Inland Sea, was a mile or so west of Kydaka Point.

The next day, with pleasant weather and a northwest wind, the two ships followed close along the shore. The journal of Thomas Manby, master's mate aboard the *Discovery*, provides the first — and very eloquent — English description of this shore:

> Never was contrast greater on this day's sailing than with what we had been long accustomed to. It had more the aspect of enchantment than reality, with silent admiration each discerned the beauties of Nature, and nought was heard on board but expressions of delight murmured from every tongue. Imperceptibly our bark skimmed over the glass surface of the deep, about three miles an hour. The shore on either side glow'd with foliage, pleasingly variegated with every shade a cheerful spring can give the forest.

Late in the afternoon, Third Lieutenant Joseph Baker of the *Discovery* observed "a very high conspicuous craggy mountain" to the east. His name was given to the mountain, the first of the many places Vancouver would name on his voyage through the Inland Sea. The ships came to anchor for the night of April 30 within the shelter of a long, low, sandy point of land. This was Dungeness Spit, which Vancouver named New Dungeness because of its resemblance to the spit by the same name in the English Channel.

The next day, May 1, Joseph Whidbey, the *Discovery*'s master, searched Dungeness Bay looking for water but found none. Vancouver, with two boats, then explored along the shore, passed Sequim Bay, and landed on Protection Island, so named by Vancouver because it could offer "fortified" protection for Port Discovery, the bay behind the island he later named for his ship. From the summit of the island, he saw a landscape "almost as enchantingly beautiful as the most elegantly furnished pleasure grounds in Europe." Discovery Island today remains largely as Vancouver described it because it is a protected bird refuge.

For Archibald Menzies, the expedition's botanist and surgeon, Protection Island was a naturalist's delight. He wrote: "It was abundantly cropped with a variety of grass clover & wild flowers, here and there adorned by aged pines with wide spreading horizontal boughs ... the whole seeming as if it had been laid out from the premeditated plan of a judicious gardener."

It was on Protection Island that he discovered the tree that bears his name, *Arbutus menziesii*, known as madroña in the United States and as arbutus in Canada.

As the expedition's only scientist, Menzies played a major role. He was selected for the role by the influential Sir Joseph Banks, president of the Royal Society. Banks, along with a staff of naturalists and artists, had sailed on Cook's first voyage to Tahiti. Banks personally prepared the instructions Menzies was to follow on the Vancouver expedition. He was to investigate "the whole of the Natural History of the countries you are to visit, as well as an enquiry into the present state & comparative degree of civilization of the inhabitants you will meet with." He was to analyze soils and climates for the possibility of future settlements and "to enumerate all the Trees, Shrubs, Plants, Grasses, Ferns, Mosses" and to bring back to England seeds and live plant specimens for propagation in London's Kew Gardens. To cultivate these plants, Menzies had an 8- by 12-foot garden box built on the after deck of the *Discovery*.

Banks also ordered that Menzies be given a boat and crew at his request, along with merchandise for trading with Native peoples.

The only minor problem of the day occurred when Thomas Manby, an ardent sportsman, shot an unfamiliar animal that turned out to be a skunk. Wrote Manby:

> In this excursion [on Protection Island] I killed a remarkable animal about the size of a cat, of a brown colour, with a large, white, bushy tail that spread over his back. After firing I approached him with all speed, and was saluted by a discharge from him the most nauseous and fetid my sense of smelling ever experienced. My gun and cloathes were so impregnated with the stench, that tho boiled in many waters the cursed effluvia could never be eradicated ... I promise faithfully never to disturb another on any consideration.

Vancouver decided that Port Discovery (now Discovery Bay), was a harbour "sufficiently secure and convenient for all our purposes ... one of the finest harbors in the world." Boat explorations found a fresh stream at the far end of the bay for the replenishment of the ships' water supply. Then the two boats returned to the ships anchored off Dungeness Spit, Vancouver feeling "perfectly satisfied with the success of our expedition, and amply rewarded for our labor." The next day, the two ships came to anchor in Port Discovery just off Carr Point.

I took my boat to the southern end of Discovery Bay and anchored. Across the swampy tidal flats, I could see traffic rushing east and west along the highway past the straggling little community of Discovery Junction. "Discovery of what?" might ask the visitor stopping briefly at this place. There is no sign, no plaque, to answer his question, but if there were, it would describe the beginning of the great two-ship, coastal-edge exploration that started out from here in May of 1792 under the command of George Vancouver.

The Lords of the Admiralty, of course, had no conception of the intricacies of the coastline Vancouver was ordered to survey. This coast, its dimensions unknown, was what lay before the expedition around the corner from Port Discovery. During the succeeding months, every mile of it would be explored and charted, capes and harbours given names, rocks and reefs noted, depths sounded and accurate locations of these features given in latitude and longitude.

At Port Discovery, work was begun to repair the two ships. Sails were mended, rigging overhauled and the hulls re-caulked. Ashore, coopers repaired barrels and the gunners dried their powder. A few men were set to brewing spruce beer. It was a concoction of spruce boughs and molasses, boiled in water and used for the prevention of scurvy, the dreaded disease of long ocean passages. Scurvy was a dietary deficiency of vitamin C. The disease first attacked the gums, causing the loss of teeth, then progressed to massive subcutaneous hemorrhaging. Death would follow as men collapsed in a condition of weakness and bodily rot. Of the 1,900 men who had sailed on the 1742 round-the-world voyage of British Admiral George Anson, 1,300 men died of scurvy.

That spruce beer must have had some effect in preventing this dreaded disease is attested to by the fact that Vancouver reported not a single case of it on his four-year voyage. Sir Joseph Banks had given Menzies the recipe for brewing spruce beer.

> Take a Copper [kettle] that contains 12 Gallons fill it
> as full of the boughs of the Black Spruce as will hold
> pressing them down pretty tight fill it up with water.
> Boil it till the Rind [bark] will strip off the Spruce

boughs which will waste it about one third take them
out & add to the water 1 gallon of Molasses. Let the
whole boil till the Molasses are dissolved. Take a half
hogshead and put in 19 Gallons of water & fill it up
with the Essence, work it with Barm [the yeast produced in making malt liquors] or Beer Grounds and
in less than a week it is fit to drink.

Though scurvy was not something that would affect me, I
wanted to see what spruce beer tasted like. I boiled some spruce
needles in water, added brown sugar, and came up with something
that tasted like sweet turpentine.

On the shore of Port Discovery, Joseph Whidbey supervised
the erection of a tent that would serve as an observatory for the
astronomical quadrant. With this instrument, the precise moment
of the sun's noon position could be observed to check the accuracy
of the ship's chronometers.

The encampment was visited by Natives who brought with them
venison and fish for trade. Vancouver was horrified when they also
offered two children for sale, a transaction he refused, "expressing
as well as I was able, our great abhorrence of such traffic." These
were the Salish-speaking Clallam First Nations. Vancouver's knowledge of the northwest-coast Aborginal culture was limited to his
contact with the Nootka people (now known as Nuu-chah-nulth)
on his previous visit to the coast with Cook. The Nootka were a
very sophisticated group which Vancouver used to compare with
the other tribal groups he encountered in the inland waters. He
soon found considerable differences between the various cultures.

All in all, his dealings with the various tribes were fair, in
accordance with his instructions from the admiralty "to use every
possible care to avoid disputes … and to conciliate their friendship

and confidence." His chief means of diplomacy came from the large inventory of trade goods he distributed as gifts.

The Aboriginal peoples the expedition encountered everywhere around the Inland Sea were extremely eager to barter food, clothing and hunting implements for such items as beads, buttons and mirrors and anything made of metal, like axes, knives and nails. More than 150 indigenous artifacts were brought back to England by the expedition and this collection was eventually acquired by the British Museum. Vancouver did not offer to trade in guns.

Menzies seemed to be more curious than Vancouver about the particular cultures and languages of the tribes they encountered, and he made a serious effort to learn a few words for each tribe. He used the clever device of seeing how each group counted, thinking this approach might provide a linguistic relationship between each group.

On May 7, Vancouver wrote:

> As our several employments, on board and on shore, would still require some time before they could be full completed; and as I was desirous of obtaining some further knowledge of this inlet, in order that, when the vessels should be ready, we might extend our research without fear of interruption, I directed the *Discovery*'s yawl and a launch, with the *Chatham*'s cutter, properly armed, and supplied with stores for five days, to be in readiness early the next morning.

And so on the morning of May 7, in fog and a moderate gale, the exploration began with the three boats setting out eastward along the southern shore of the strait, keeping, as Vancouver wrote, the "continental shore to the right." This tactic, mainland always to the right, was the simple and infallible method adopted by Vancouver for his survey of the continental edge. It also provided a constantly reliable method for the boats to find their way back from the intricacies of the coast to the anchored mother ships. This method can be illustrated by the idea of a blind man entering through a doorway into a house. Were he to walk blindly around that house, in and out of each room, touching the walls to his right as he walked, he would eventually return to the doorway of his beginning.

Mainland to the right brought the expedition to Point Wilson, and more than two centuries later I followed that little flotilla along that shore in my boat on an equally foggy morning. My eyes told me nothing and I had to guess my distance from the unseen shore as I followed along the outside edge of the kelp-line, which I hoped would keep me clear of rocks. The silence around me was broken only by the sounds of the sea: the hollow tumbling of the surf as it washed and rolled the stones on the unseen beach and the offshore rushing of deep water streaming to the sea.

Fog erased all concepts of time. I could imagine the blurred outline of a ship's boat, see men bent to the stroke of their wet, dripping oars. They were going where no white man had ever been, to places never mapped, places — for them — without names. What, I wondered, would be their perceptions of time and distance in the slow, laborious day-to-day explorations they made through these tangled waters as they rowed and sailed on and on through unknown distances and unexpected hazards, through wind and rain and storm. And it was here, imagining those huddled shapes in the fog, that I first asked, "Could I have been one of them?"

As the weather cleared, the bay that Vancouver named Port Townshend (after Brigadier-General Marquis Townshend) opened to the south. To the southeast "a very remarkable high round mountain was observed," which he named Mount Rainier (honouring Admiral

Peter Rainier). Three waterways opened from the view at Point Wilson: Admiralty Inlet (named for England's Board of Admiralty), Port Townsend Bay and Kilisut Harbor lying between Marrowstone (a type of stone noted there) and Indian islands. Johnstone went into Kilisut Harbor, Puget down the centre of Port Townsend Bay and Vancouver along the mainland shore. Vancouver's way was blocked at the southern end of the bay by a low, sandy isthmus (now cut by the Port Townsend Canal). Vancouver and Puget stopped to eat together in the lower end of Port Townsend Bay, and here the romantic young Manby, a friend of the aristocratic Townshend family, expressed his affection for a Townshend daughter by carving her name on a tree. His inscription read:

> The next visitor to this remote region should he by accident saunter to the plain, may have his curiosity attracted by the same object that drew mine: a clump formed by five prodigious cypress trees. On one, the most stately of the number, I carved with my knife Ann Marie Townshend and under it T.M. 1792 and whoever thou are, traveler, know that she possesses every beauty as a woman this unequalled cypress does as a tree, without fault or blemish, a pattern to the world of goodness and a virtuous sole.

(My history resources did not reveal whether or not young Manby later married his Ann Marie.)

Johnstone drew the unlucky assignment. His course took him to the sand-spit-blocked end of Kilisut Harbour and back, and it was not until the next morning, after rowing most of the night, that he was able to rejoin the other two boats at the rendezvous of Marrowstone Island.

Opposing tide and wind slowed the three boats as they explored south through Admiralty Inlet the next day, and it was not until 1:00 a.m. the following morning, in a drenching rainstorm, that a landing was made in Oak Bay (named after the Garry oak trees there). In this camp — and in the many to follow — tents were erected for the officers but the crews had no covering except for wet clothes and sails. Vancouver's health was later to suffer from such exposed encampments, but no other commander of a nautical survey took such an active, personal part in the work, essentially suffering the same hardships as his crews. The weather on May 9 held the flotilla stormbound in the Oak Bay camp. During the enforced idleness, clams were gathered at low tide and berries picked in the woods.

A strong southeast wind and an ebb tide again opposed the three boats as they moved south from Oak Cove on May 10. Two openings appeared ahead: Hood Canal (after Vice-Admiral Lord Hood) and the continuation of Admiralty Inlet, separated by the point Vancouver named Foulweather Bluff because of the adverse weather experienced in the area. All three boats proceeded south through Hood Canal to Hazel Point and then around the perimeter of Dabob Bay to Quatsap Point, where camp was made.

May 12 was the fifth day of a voyage that had supplies for only five days, and the food was nearly exhausted. Hunting had produced no game and trading with Natives, little food. Vancouver wrote this rather dismal description of Hood Canal:

> The region we had lately passed seemed nearly destitute of human beings. The brute creation also had deserted the shores; the tracks of deer were no longer to be seen; nor was there an aquatic bird on the whole extent of the canal; animated nature seemed

nearly exhausted; and her awful silence was only now and then interrupted by the croaking of a raven, the breathing of a seal or the scream of an eagle. Even these solitary sounds were so seldom heard, that the rustling of the breeze along the shore, assisted by the solemn stillness that prevailed, gave rise to ridiculous suspicions in our seamen of hearing rattlesnakes, and other hideous monsters, in the wilderness.

I followed the boats down Hood Canal and it was largely as Vancouver described it: depressing. I thought its waters flat and lifeless and the shoreline marred by the tacky houses and small communities that straddled the highway running along the west shore of the canal. And "hideous monsters" *do* exist in Hood Canal in the form of the long, grey submarines docked at the Bangor naval base, each boat equipped with enough atomic bombs to destroy most of the world.

Though short of food, Vancouver decided to complete the survey of Hood Canal "at the expense of a little hunger," for he carried on to the southern end of the canal at the Great Bend. From there, Johnstone went ahead a few miles to explore eastward to where the inlet ended. He did not realize that the southern end of Hood Canal was less than two miles distant from the head of Case Inlet in Puget Sound, which a few days later would be explored by Puget.

While Johnstone was away, Vancouver met with a large group of Twana First Nations off Ayers Point who received him with "cordiality, and treated him with marks of great friendship and hospitality." His camp for the night was probably in Dewatto Bay.

On May 13, the flotilla headed back up Hood Canal against a stiff northwest wind toward Foulweather Bluff. In deteriorating weather, another camp was made in Hood Canal, probably in the area of Misery Point across from the opening of Dabob Bay. Foulweather Bluff was reached in the afternoon of May 14, "a promontory not ill named," commented Vancouver, "for we had scarcely landed, when a heavy rain commenced, which continuing the rest of the day, obliged us to remain stationary."

I, too, became stormbound at Foulweather Bluff, but in conditions vastly different than those endured by Vancouver and his men. My own journal for the night reads:

> Hard rain drums on the cabin roof, and the wind moans through the tight rigging as the boat rolls in the surge of the waves. But I am thoroughly enjoying this night as I sit in the boat's small cabin, warmed by the steady soft purr of the kerosene stove. Games of solitaire with well-worn cards fill a few hours of the early evening, but then, as the glass of rum empties, I turn to writing. My pen crosses the pages of my notebook leaving behind words that describe that other night of storm over two centuries ago when three small boats and their crews had sought shelter on this point. Would I really want to have been one of them? My answer to that question might lie in the night I remember during another storm. I had been walking along the river shore close to my home. Far out in the river, the faint loom of an island was just visible through falling snow. I stood and watched the island until its outline disappeared in the darkness of the winter evening and wondered what it would be like to be out on the island in the storm. I imagined myself crouched in some crude shelter before a fire, the snow piling up around me, the wind moaning

through the bare trees. I imagined myself out there sitting at the elemental edge of something not at all frightening or threatening. Just me, alone by a fire in a night scene of storm. I, the person I thought myself to be, would be of no importance and absent. Another self — a more primitive me — would watch the fire, ears alert listening to the sounds of the wind. I would settle down within myself, adjust my body to the cold hard ground, clasp arms and hands across my chest and hold within me the core of myself, an imagined centre of heat I would draw on to survive the night as I waited with passionate anticipation for something as simple as the dawn.

And I am sure that Vancouver's men, after enduring their long night of dark and rain, would have shared my "passionate anticipation for something as simple as the dawn."

The same weather imprisoned the men during the next day at Foulweather Bluff and it was not until the afternoon of May 15 — in "heavy squalls and torrents of rain" — that the three boats with the men, tired, hungry, wet and cold and now three days overdue, made it back to the ships anchored in Port Discovery.

On this eight-day expedition, Vancouver had surveyed 175 coastal miles and the results of this survey were drawn on the preliminary plotting sheet from which the chart of the overall coast was later drawn. The survey method used during this first exploration — and repeated over and over again as the boats charted the twists and turns of the mainland coast — was called a "running survey." It called for the boats to be rowed along the shoreline as compass bearings were taken on prominent land features. More accurate bearings of coastal features were taken from shore positions by sextant angles. When clear skies permitted, noon observations were made each day to obtain latitude and longitude at various locations. The process was slow and tedious, but its cumulative information, obtained over the course of many miles and many boat expeditions, eventually outlined the mainland shore of the Inland Sea.

After following this stretch of the survey, I made a dash back from the miserable weather of the bluff to Port Townsend. The weather cleared as I rounded Marrowstone Point and there, ahead of me, was the old city looking as a seaport should to a sailor wanting a sheltered harbour: a waterfront of sheds, docks and boats and behind this, a street of brick buildings that promised the pleasures of the shore. For a century and a half, Port Townsend has watched the ebb and flow of history and the coming and going of ships and men. Mostly, the going.

When it was founded in 1851, the city had every reason to believe it would become the major port of Puget Sound. It was 70 miles closer to the ocean than that upstart city of Seattle. Behind its capacious harbour stood an apparently inexhaustible source of timber and, in San Francisco, there was an inexhaustible demand for its lumber.

In the late 1850s, the Fraser River gold rush drew thousands of men to British Columbia, and Port Townsend was where many of the miners were outfitted. James McCurdy, in his book *By Juan de Fuca's Strait*, recreated what one of those miners might have encountered as he stepped ashore at Port Townsend during that feverish time:

In leaving his vessel, he trod a spindly dock that threatened to collapse under the strain of the traffic it had never been designed to sustain. As he wandered about the primitive settlement, many scenes would be unfolded that would probably remain indefinitely in his memory ... the straggling row of houses maintaining their precarious footing along the edge of a lofty eminence; a road running up the face of the bluff, so steep that no horse would climb it without the stimulation of a whip; the sinuous lagoon, with its stagnant pools and aroma of decayed vegetation; the curious zigzag incline, by which pedestrians gained the residential plateau; sandy roads full of ruts, miscellaneous stocks of goods in flimsy frame buildings along the one business street; evil-smelling saloons ... gambling dens where sums sufficient to buy half the town exchanged hands daily ... soldiers, sailors and Indians, in picturesque garb ... the street throngs ... singing, swearing and dancing ... and mongrel dogs constantly under foot.

One visitor, writes McCurdy, while strolling with one of the city's founders, noted the raw town's scenic backdrop of forest and sea and said the place looked like a "cheap jewel in a setting of gold." "Give us time," said the townsman, "and we will have a city here none may feel ashamed of."

And prosper it did, for a time, not as a rough frontier boomtown, but as an elegant city of Victorian-style brick and stone buildings and houses. At the peak of its prosperity in the 1880s, Port Townsend had a main street lined with buildings that housed banks, a customs house, the city hall, the county court house and numerous thriving stores. Seven miles of railroad track had been

laid on a line that was to tie Port Townsend to the trans-contin-
ental system. That vital connection was never made and the city,
caught in a whirlwind of land speculation in the late 1880s, all but
collapsed. Population dropped from 7,000 citizens to fewer than
2,000. Olympia, Tacoma and Seattle got the railroad (and Seattle
the boom years of the Alaska gold rush). Port Townsend, isolated
by the sea that was to make it a world port, died in the century in
which it had been born.

The railroad still does not come to Port Townsend, but tourists
do, and the town's history has given it an economic and cultural
revival. Its themes were everywhere as I walked the city's main
street through crowds wearing the tennis-shoes, jeans and T-shirt
uniforms of summer visitors. The entire downtown area has been
declared a National Historic District, and within it are 70 buildings and homes that have been restored as showcases of Victorian
architecture and craftsmanship. These century-old buildings house
antique stores, art galleries, restaurants, gift shops and — here and
there — an honest working man's saloon for fishermen, boat build-
ers, loafers and ne'er-do-wells. The Port Townsend Wooden Boat
Festival has been raised to the status of a cult with people coming
from all over the northwest to ooh and aah at the varnished wood
and polished brass of wooden boats that, like the city itself, conjure
up a vision of former elegance and style.

This is history cleaned up, sanitized, pasteurized. No town
drunks or sailors stagger along sidewalks, no impolite smells
emanate from outhouses hanging over the seawall. This is history
as a commodity, a consumer product that can be sold as fun. And
fun it is, for the people walking up and down the sidewalks, eating
"homemade" ice cream and shopping for souvenirs and antiques.

But history in a place like Port Townsend, I think, can have a
deeper meaning, one that can fulfil a nostalgic yearning to return

— if only for a day or two — to that sentimental vision of something called "better days." Formal history — the kind drummed into our heads at school — tries to teach us to lay aside illusion and make-believe, and replace them with historic reality.

Reality: flat, aimless and boring. What history can be is a stage setting for an escape from a ho-hum present. Port Townsend is such a setting, expressing through its refurbished history a picture of how we like to think things might have been. We can fill the picture with the scenery, the actors and a script of our imagination to recreate a time that seems to have had something our time has lost. An old-timer I spoke to in Port Townsend said that the best thing about the old days was that they were gone. Perhaps he was right, but again, I wonder.

In those bygone days, people were a minority influence along the shores of this Inland Sea, their lives dominated by an all-power-ful nature. Their role was to somehow eke out a living from that nature by taming it, cultivating and civilizing it. It was not glam-orous; no romance can be attached to the hoe, the pick, the axe, the oar, the back-breaking, crippling work, the incurable diseases, the isolation, the wet and the mud. That was reality in the good old days. But there was a hardscrabble purpose to life back then that perhaps made each day endurable because of the belief that somehow, tomorrow — through hard work, a little luck and a lot of faith — would be better. Port Townsend built itself on that dream. The dream failed but we can go there today to recall its vision: a vision of what its pioneer citizens believed was possible.

Making history come alive; Port Townsend does it with old buildings and wooden boats. I do it by retracing an 18th-century sailing expedition in my boat. We are equally guilty of romanti-cizing a past that both of us feel is perhaps more interesting than the present.

In Port Discovery, discipline — as in most cases when a ship was either in port or lying at anchor — had become somewhat lax during Vancouver's absence. Three men had been punished by Joseph Baker, who had been left in charge: one man with 12 lashes for insolence to his superior officer; another man, 18 lashes for the same offence; and 24 lashes to a third man for both insolence and drunkenness. This form of punishment in the British navy of the period was the accepted and expected punishment for wrongdoing. Naval historian N. A. Rogers points out in his book *An Anatomy of the Georgian Navy* that rigid discipline aboard a ship was something inherent in seafaring. He writes:

> Discipline created the collective condition of a crew that made its members capable of handling duties and responsibilities. Discipline was not so much a hand-ed-down set of rules by officers but, rather, a code mutually accepted by seamen. Discipline enforced that code and seamen knew that orders had to be obeyed for the safety of all ... The duty of the officers was to impose it, the duty of the crew to accept it.

Flogging was punishment by the rules and it "was over in the doing of it," says Greg Dening in *Mr. Bligh's Bad Language*. Sailors, he writes: "... liked the fact that flogging left no doubt ... it was not something done in revenge or for retribution. It was objective, done purely to make an example ... Flogging should never be done in anger ... The occasion should immediately be expunged from memory."

The lash was not spared aboard the *Discovery* or the *Chatham*. Vancouver was frequently arbitrary, rigid and given to outbursts of temper and violence. Punishment for minor misdemeanours resulted in three to four dozen lashes. The most frequent offences were drunkenness, neglect of duty, insolence, fighting and theft. Some 45 such punishments were ordered aboard the *Discovery* during the 10-month period between February and November 1792. Sentences of 24 lashes were common but some punishments called for 36 and even 48 lashes. The most frequently flogged man aboard the *Discovery* was George Reybold, who was given 252 lashes on nine different occasions. During the same period, 21 floggings were ordered aboard the *Chatham*. If the punishment was excessive, so, too, were the conditions that made it so: long months of cold, uncomfortable duty unrelieved by shore leave or any break in the rigid monotony of shipboard life.

Aboard *Kea*, however inept Dumbshit was, he was never punished this severely by the captain.

VII.

The San Juan Islands

AFTER TWO DAYS WALKING AROUND PORT TOWNSEND, I WAS ready to rejoin the Vancouver expedition that on May 18 departed from Port Discovery, its casks filled with fresh water, rigging overhauled and the chronometer accurately set on Greenwich time.

Broughton in the *Chatham* was sent to investigate a group of islands to the northwest (the San Juan Islands) while Vancouver turned south through Admiralty Inlet and sailed along the edge of Whidbey Island, later named by him for Joseph Whidbey, the *Discovery*'s master. Vancouver projected "the first inlet to the southeastward [of Foulweather Bluff] on the starboard or continental shore as our place of rendezvous." (Here is shown the simplicity of the "mainland to the right" concept which allowed a rendezvous point to be established at a distant point not yet seen.)

A strong ebb tide forced the *Discovery* to anchor some 24 miles down Admiralty Inlet off Whidbey Island. The next day, the fore-topsail yard broke and the spare yard was found to be defective. "It was," wrote Vancouver, "a very fortunate circumstance, that these defects were discovered in a country abounding with materials to which we could resort; having only to make our choice among thousands of the finest spars the world produces."

It was here that Vancouver wrote admiringly, "To describe the beauties of this region, will, on some future occasion, be a very grateful task to the pen of a skillful panegyrist."

Vancouver turned south into Puget Sound, later named for Peter Puget who first explored its waters, and anchored his ship off Restoration Point on Bainbridge Island. The name of the point commemorated the restoration of the English crown after the fall of Oliver Cromwell on May 25, 1660. During the next few days, while they awaited the *Chatham*, new spars were cut. Vancouver and Joseph Baker went through narrow Rich Passage to Port Orchard, which had been discovered by Vancouver's clerk, H. M. Orchard. Vancouver described it as "a most complete and excellent port." (Apparently, the U.S. Navy shares his assessment of Port Orchard, since its huge Bremerton shipyard is located there.)

Meanwhile, Broughton in the *Chatham*, in company with Johnstone in a cutter, had been exploring the complicated channels of the San Juan Islands. They had already been explored by Spain's Francisco Eliza, who named the group Isla y Archipelago de San Juan on June 21, 1791, to honour the birthdate of St. John the Baptist. By this name, and the others Eliza left behind in the San Juans, is Spain remembered in these waters: Lopez, Orcas, Guemes, Patos and Sucia were all at one time considered by Spain as its island possessions.

Broughton spent seven days exploring the San Juan group. "The Land," wrote his clerk, Edward Bell, "is delightful, being in many places clear and the Soil so rich that the grass in several parts grew to man height." Broughton's journal provides a very utilitarian survey of the islands, noting only the locations of major islands and the compass directions and depths of its complicated channels. A detailed exploration was considered unnecessary because the archipelago was not a part of the mainland shore that was Vancouver's primary survey focus. Broughton did not name any of the islands.

On a glorious summer morning, I began to travel from east to west through the San Juan group, which consists of 468 islands and minor rocks and 373 miles of shoreline. Low fog, rolling in from Rosario Strait, tailed me through Thatcher Pass. Clouds hung over the top of Mount Constitution on Orcas but the lower hills of the islands stood out like domes of green. The narrow channels of Wasp and Pole passages, with their layers of rock, madroña and pine stretching along the shore edge of the sea, were so lovely that, turning the boat around, I ran the passages again.

That night, I anchored in the little bay on the north side of Jones Island. I had gone to the island many years ago in a kayak. There are places in the world that one visits and never forgets, and Jones Island, for me, was one of those places.

I had pitched my tent on a small rocky point of the island that looked over the sea bordered by the pine- and madroña-clad shoreline. It was a scenery altogether new to me, a meeting line of shore and sea in black rock and blue water that seemed to match some dreamscape of mine, a kind of composite image of a rocky Maine coastline and a green tropical island. I had never seen the Maine coastline or a tropical island, but Jones Island, in my mind, expressed the images of both places. I left the island after only one night there, not knowing at the time that it would be etched in my memory as an idealized landscape of an island and the sea. The pleasure of returning to Jones Island after so many years was to find that it looked as I remembered it, that it still gave me that sense of a discovered place and would forever be both reality and memory.

The next day, I sailed past the bare, summer-browned slopes of Spieden Island and south through Mosquito Pass to Garrison Bay on San Juan Island to visit the site of an interesting historical event of the Inland Sea, one that nearly precipitated a war between England and the United States.

In 1860, British Royal Marines established a post at Garrison Bay to assert England's claim to the San Juan Islands. The United States also claimed the islands and established a post at the southern end of San Juan. Both nations were responding to the controversial shooting of an American farmer's pig by an English farmer. For the next 11 years, while the United States and Great Britain argued about the ownership of the island, the two armies occupied their respective armed camps, slowly forgetting that they had been sent there to fight each other as they picnicked together, competed in races, celebrated mutual holidays and, on Sundays, jointly hosted visitors who crossed over to the island from Victoria.

Today, the site of the home built for the commanding officers of the British camp overlooks a restored, eight-sided formal garden of clipped hedges enclosed by a white picket fence and surrounded by a spacious green lawn. Walking around that garden, it was easy for me to imagine a scene that could have happened any sunny Sunday afternoon at the fort in the 1860s. From the cricket match in the far corner of the field, the crack of a bat is followed by gloved applause as a run is scored. In another corner, tea is being served under the shade of a striped canvas pavilion, pennants fluttering from its supporting poles. And around the garden, arm in arm, stroll uniformed officers and their wives, nodding greetings as they circle the garden. This trim, neat military post was the last corner of the continental United States to be occupied by foreign troops, posted here to fight a war that never happened.

The disputed ownership of the San Juan Islands was finally submitted to Kaiser William I of Germany who — perhaps to spite his cousin Queen Victoria — ruled in favour of the United States by establishing Haro Strait as the dividing line between the United States and Canada. By this decision, the United States acquired the islands.

VIII.

Puget's Sound

THE NEXT PHASE OF VANCOUVER'S EXPLORATION WOULD TAKE *Kea* and me into our home waters: the 200-mile shoreline and the eight long inlets of Puget Sound. I was familiar with its many coves and bays but looked forward to adding the story of its first exploration to what I knew about the sound by following Peter Puget's six-day boat voyage around its perimeter.

Boats were used because the complexities of the shore he had traced so far convinced Vancouver that the two large ships would be too unwieldy for the continuation of the survey. Anchored at Restoration Point he wrote:

> On due consideration of all the circumstances that had fallen under my own observation, and the intelligence now imparted by Mr. Broughton, I became

thoroughly convinced, that our boats alone could enable us to acquire any correct or satisfactory information respecting this broken country; and although the execution of such a service in open boats would necessarily be extremely laborious, and expose those so employed to numberless dangers and unpleasant situations, that might occasionally produce great fatigue, and protract their return to the ship; yet that mode was undoubtedly the most accurate, the most ready, and indeed the only one in our power to pursue for ascertaining the continental boundary.

This decision determined the future of the survey. The role of the two ships would to be find safe anchorages, where water and wood were available, and from there the boat expeditions would be sent out. For the boat crews, this new tactic would mean long days in adverse conditions of rain, wind and cold, and nights camped ashore or sometimes in the boats when they could not make a landing.

Archibald Menzies described the conditions endured by Peter Puget, Joseph Whidbey, himself and their men on the six-day exploration of Puget Sound:

The weather was now become so cold wet & uncomfortable that the men were no longer able to endure the fatiguing hardships in open boats exposed to the cold rigorous blasts of a high northern situation with high dreary snowy mountains on every side, performing toilsome labor on their oars in the day, & alternately watching for their own safety at night, with no other couch to repose upon than the Cold Stony Beach or the wet mossy Turf in deep wood situations, without having shelter sufficient to screen them from the inclemency of the boisterous weather, & enduring at times the tormenting pangs of both hunger and thirst.

Each boat was manned by an officer, a midshipman, a few marines and the rowing crew. The boats were armed with small swivel cannons and muskets, and each carried a variety of trade items for barter with the Natives. Vancouver had been ordered "to use every possible care to avoid disputes with the natives ... and by a judicious distribution of the presents ... to conciliate their friendship and confidence." Puget wrote that barter was conducted "with the Strictest honesty on both Sides ... for we would never accept any Article till the Owner was satisfied with what was offered in Exchange."

The food provided on these boat expeditions consisted of wheat, dried soup and spirits, cooked in large copper pots. The soup, previously prepared in England, was a mix of vegetables and the internal organs of oxen. It was boiled to make a pulp that was then dried and cut into slabs. On numerous occasions, the boats stayed out beyond the time for which they had been provisioned, and the men had to augment their food by trade with Aboriginal people and by gathering berries, shooting birds and fishing. Puget mentioned that "the People were not averse to eating Crows of which we could always procure plenty." Two cooked meals were served each day when conditions permitted, one in the morning and the other at the end of the day, a working day that would begin at dawn and last until sunset. Certainly, the success of the survey expedition must be attributed in a large part to the men who took part in the boat expeditions. Menzies gave them unqualified praise:

It is impossible silently to pass over so hard and Laborious an Undertaking as the Duty of the Boats, without [noting] that indefatigable exertion and Attention that has on all Occasions been paid by the Officer under whose Direction they were conducted and also the Seamen who performed the Laborious task of the Oar. At this they frequently labored from Morning till Night & allways performed that Duty with alacrity, not even a Murmur was heard. Necessity obliged us frequently to pull till Eleven at Night, which Still made no difference in the Hour of Departure.

Rowing morning to night, eating crows, sleeping in open boats ... well, I did these things when I was younger (except for eating crows), so I have some sense of what those men endured. What separates us is not the physical conditions but the mental outlook. I knew where I was, where I was going, and that I could quit at any time of my choosing. They had no such choices, and that is the unbridgeable difference between my own boat voyage through the sound and theirs.

In all, some 40 boat expeditions were sent out to survey the coast with Vancouver participating in many of them at the expense of his health. The seaworthiness of the boats used on these expeditions also contributed to the success of the survey. They were more or less a stock design built for the Royal Navy: the *Chatham*'s cutter and launch were 22 and 19 feet in length; the *Discovery*'s boats were around 24 feet long. The boats would normally be rowed by six pairs of oars, double banked, with two men on each thwart pulling one oar apiece. The sailing rig was a two-masted lug rig, loose footed. The seaworthiness of the cutters is attested to by the remarkable voyage of Captain William Bligh, who used such a boat to carry his 18 men across 3,600 miles of open sea after they were forced to leave their ship, the *Bounty*, which had been commandeered by Fletcher Christian.

Puget and Whidbey in the launch and cutter with a week's provisions departed May 20 to explore the shoreline of the eight long inlets of what would later be named Puget's Sound. Menzies, always eager to extend his botanical studies, joined them. Out of that voyage by sail and oar the history of the sound began with this entry written by Puget: "Early in the Morning we left the Ships with two Boats well Armed, the Launch carried two Swivels besides Musquetoons & Musquettes & provided with a Weeks Provisions we began the examination of the Inlet."

This was Colvos Passage lying west of Vashon Island (named after Admiral James Vashon). This island was the only place in the lower sound named by Vancouver. The passage carried the boats through the tidal currents of Point Defiance and The Narrows, where, wrote Puget, "A most Rapid Tide from the Northward hurried us so fast past the Shore that we could scarce land."

All the tidal waters flowing in and out of southern Puget Sound race through the four-mile-long Narrows. *Kea* is stopped by this current when running against it and is tossed and turned by the swirling currents when running with it. Therefore, I can imagine that it must have been a frightening experience for the men in two rowboats to be suddenly swept through this tidal race without knowing where it was carrying them or where it would end.

Natives in two canoes appeared at the end of passage, and Puget attempted to engage them with what he thought would be the "Signs emblematical of friendship, such as a Handkerchief [but] a Green Bough & many other Methods [would not] induce them to venture near us, on the Contrary, it appeared to have another Effect, that of redoubling their Efforts in getting away."

Keeping the mainland to the right, the boats then turned north-westerly through Hale Passage and into Woolochet Bay just inside Point Fosdick, where other Natives were encountered, drying clams and fish, which they traded for buttons and beads. Puget described them as slender, long-haired and naked with copper ornaments hanging from perforated ears and noses. These were members of the Squaxin tribe, who today still fish these waters and provide me with the fresh salmon and clams I cook aboard *Kea*.

In the afternoon, another group of Natives appeared. Puget, "apprehensive they would be endeavoring to commit Depredations during the Night ordered a Musquette to be fired but ... they remained stationary, only exclaiming Pop at every Report in a way of Derision ... they however soon after left us, nor did they trouble us afterwards."

The expedition continued along the mainland shore behind Fox Island to its first camp on Green Point in lower Carr Inlet after travelling 26 miles.

On the second day of the expedition, in rain and against an opposing tide, the boats worked up to the head of Carr Inlet, passing "an astonishing Quantity of Crows" on Raft Island (the crows are still there). Twenty armed Natives met the men when they stopped along the western shore of Carr Inlet. Puget drew a line in the sand to separate the two parties, which the Natives did not cross though they showed a "distrustful Behaviour." Other groups in canoes appeared and landed on the beach, stringing their bows and "apparently preparing for an Attack." This, wrote Puget, "reduced me to a most awkward predicament, for unwilling to fire on the poor People, who might have been unacquainted with the advantage we had over them & not wishing to run the Risk of having the [our] People wounded by the first discharge of their Arrows I absolutely felt at a Loss how to Act."

It was a tense moment. If Puget did nothing, a first attack by the Natives could seriously wound his men. He directed one of the swivel cannons to be harmlessly shot as a warning but "contrary to our Expectation they did not express any Astonishment or fear at the Report or the Effect of the Shot." Finally, with his men standing fully armed, the Natives "totally relinquished all Idea of an Attack for they now offered their Bow and Arrows for Sale ... and Solicited our Friendship by the most abject submission and we had the Satisfaction of having convinced them of our Friendship." This was the only instance during Vancouver's entire survey when any of his men were confronted by hostile Natives. The site of this encounter was probably Von Geldern Cove, halfway down the west shoreline of Key Peninsula at the entrance to the community of Home.

In deteriorating weather, the expedition continued down Carr Inlet to a campsite on the shore of narrow Pitt Passage. On the third day of the voyage, the boats went through Pitt Passage, then Balch Pass and across to a landing on Ketron Island. A fierce squall drove the men from the island and they crossed over the main sound to camp in Oro Bay at the lower end of Anderson Island.

On the morning of May 23, dense fog delayed the departure from Oro Bay. Puget suspected that the broad lowland of Nisqually Flats contained a river outlet, but no landing was made to confirm this hunch because of the shallow water off the flats. Trading with Natives on this day was peaceful. The course for the day carried the boats up Case Inlet, where another storm with torrential rains drove the men to a camp on Herron Island.

On May 24, 15-mile-long Case Inlet was explored. The inlet ends at a narrow, two-mile wide isthmus, crossed by a road and an old Aboriginal portage trail leading to the lower end of Hood Canal, previously explored by Johnstone. Turning, the boats came down the west shore of Case Inlet to the opening of Pickering Passage and then down this passage, lying between Hartstene Island and the mainland shore. The men camped on the mainland near the southern end of Pickering Passage after a 12-hour day at the oars.

From this camp, Puget was able to look down Peale Passage running between Hartstene and Squaxin islands, a passage he thought would return him to the main branch of the sound. Probably at this point, Puget was eager to conclude his survey. None of the long inlets he had explored led to any significant passages, his men were tired and his food supply was running low. What the view down Peale Passage did not reveal was the complicated maze of inlets and long peninsulas that compose the lower sound: Totten, Eld, Budd and Henderson inlets with a shoreline of more than 50 miles.

For more than a year I had been wandering the ins and outs of these inlets, but it took a number of explorations before I could travel them with the confidence of knowing where I was without reference to my chart. What Puget did to unravel this skein of long, narrow arms was to follow the simple wisdom of Vancouver's command: "Keep the mainland to the right." Hammersley Inlet was passed without exploration, and by noon, the boats had reached the southern end of Totten Inlet. In this branch, Puget observed, "were many beautiful Spots the Low Surrounding Country though thickly covered with Wood had a very pleasant Appearance, now in the height of Spring." Camp for this night was made on Cooper Point at the junction of Eld and Budd inlets. In one long, tedious day, these inlets were explored by oar. Each was probably approached with the anticipation of discovering something of particular interest, but both ended in shallow swamps and from there the men had to row back along a shoreline they had already seen.

Puget did name Eld Inlet "Friendly Inlet" because in landing, the men "were received by the Inhabitants with all the Friendship and Hospitality we could have expected." Women seen were curing clams and fish and weaving watertight, colourful baskets, while the men fished and built canoes. At that Aboriginal village, Puget wrote: "The only Difference I perceived between our present Companions and former visitors, were the Extravagance with Which their Faces were Ornamented." He described this ornamentation as red ochre and "black glimmer" with hair covered with bird feathers.

After completing the surveys of Eld and Budd inlets, the expedition went through Dana Passage to a final camp on Johnson Point at the entrance to Henderson Inlet. From there, the return trip of 50 miles to the anchored *Discovery* at Restoration Point took 22 hours of rowing and sailing. Deservedly were the waters Puget explored named after him.

While Puget and Whidbey were surveying the lower sound, Vancouver and Lieutenant Joseph Baker had made a three-day voyage that took them down East Passage east of Vashon Island, then southeast through the sound probably as far as Johnson Point at the tip of Henderson Inlet. Assuming correctly that Puget had explored the shoreline beyond this point, Vancouver returned to his ship. Thus, by sail and oar, the unknown waters of Puget Sound were surveyed and named. Vancouver predicted the future of the sound: "The serenity of the climate, the innumerable pleasing landscapes and the abundant fertility that unassisted nature puts forth, required only to be enriched by the industry of man ... to render it the most lovely country that can be imagined."

Whidbey was less sanguine. He thought the lower sound too far distant from any place of importance to be of any future value except as a drop-off site for those English prisoners who had served out their time in Australia's penal colony at Botany Bay but should not be allowed to return to England. Vancouver, however, rightly prophesied the future of the sound and, in 1833, the Hudson's Bay Company founded the Puget Sound Agricultural Company at Fort Nisqually, the first white settlement on the sound. The company began as a storehouse and a few crude huts for the men, surrounded by a protective palisade of pointed logs. There was a small herd of cattle from California and a few sheep from England. In a few years, the herds of cattle and sheep had multiplied to thousands on the company's 167,000 acres of grazing land.

Were I to try to land on any of Puget's campsites today, I would probably find myself trespassing on someone's front lawn. Who owns the shoreline of Puget Sound and other Washington state shores is a controversial issue that pits private landowners against the increased number of people who want public access to the beaches and islands of the sound.

In the last few years, the state and federal agencies have set aside over 150 shore areas and islands for public use along the Washington coast of the Inland Sea. It is not enough, but it is a marked improvement over the time when the state sold title to most of its saltwater shorelines.

The first settlers of these shores could not claim ownership because they were publicly owned by the state of Washington. That ownership was derived from the land-use laws based on the English legal system adopted by the 13 founding American colonies. It declared that the shores of navigable waters — up to the line of ordinary high tide — was property owned by the colonies and not individuals. Each new state retained this ownership, including Washington when it was admitted to the union in 1889.

With the state owning the shoreline, settlers did not have legal access across it for fishing, transportation or water-based industries, so, in 1890, the state legislature authorized the sale of its public tidelands to individuals. It was not until 1971 that this practice was discontinued, but by then most of the public shoreline had been sold.

This loss of public beach access to residential and commercial development, and the abuse and overuse of some saltwater resources such as clams and oysters, prompted a turn-about in the early 1970s with the adoption of the Shoreline Management Act that gave the state broad control over the development and use of the shoreline. The preservation of the shoreline's natural character was the objective of the act and, today, state parks and wildlife refuges have returned to public use hundreds of miles of shore, islands and natural habitat areas.

As a result, when I traced Puget's voyage around the perimeter of the sound, I was constantly surprised to see so much of the shoreline looking much the same as he saw it. Of course there are many changes: concentrations of homes, marinas, industrial buildings and two major cities. I found that by squinting a little, I could visually edit the scene in my view — ignore a particularly large house or a small clear-cut and imagine two boats with their rowing crews silently crossing a misty inlet. An inlet still there in all its beauty and mysteries for *Kea* and me to explore.

IX.

Possession Sound

IN FOLLOWING PUGET THROUGH THE SOUND, MY COURSES HAD wandered through all the directions of the compass as I made short tacks up and down the inlets. I was now eager to sail more open waters as I followed Vancouver up through the upper reaches of Puget Sound, Admiralty Inlet and Rosario Strait.

On May 30, the *Discovery* left Restoration Point and headed north. He passed a wide bay on the mainland shore, which he thought "only an indentation of the shore." This was Elliott Bay, future site of Seattle. The city came into my view when I rounded Alki Point as a burnished cluster of geometric shapes, humming with the life of a great city greeting the day. Why, I wondered, was this great city founded here on a bay described by Vancouver as an unimportant indentation of the shore?

The city is here, say legend and history, because on the wet, cold morning of November 13, 1851, 10 adults and 12 children landed on Alki Point, and out of that first group emerged what would become the "Queen City" of the sound.

One man, a Yukon Native, had much to do with Seattle winning that coveted title. His name was Skookum Jim. On the morning of August 17, 1896, Jim discovered gold in the icy waters of Bonanza Creek, a tributary of the Klondike River. What followed was the Yukon gold rush. A year later, the first Klondike prospectors arrived in Seattle on the steamship *Portland*. The captain telegraphed ahead with a message that said the ship was carrying a ton of gold.

Thousands were there to greet the ship as it docked, many of them immediately booking passage on the *Portland* for the return trip to Alaska. The news was wired around the world, and with it the "get rich quick" stories of prospectors who had only to lean over to gather nuggets.

"Clondyke," reported one Seattle newspaper, "is almost a household word. In every city, town and hamlet on the Pacific Coast little else is talked of and people are preparing to go north by the first means of transportation they can encounter."

By the thousands they came to Seattle and left for the north in anything that would float. Most made nothing, but Seattle's merchants, shipbuilders and outfitters made fortunes. The fever did not last long, but it was long enough to get Seattle through the depression years of the 1890s and it entered the new century with a newly built port and railroad facilities ready to serve not only Alaska, but the world.

And I, like those miners on their way to Alaska, stopped off in Seattle just long enough to outfit the boat for the voyage ahead: fresh vegetables from the Pike Street Market, a wool shirt from a second-hand clothing store and a tank of fuel. Then I headed across the sound, entered Rich Passage and went up to the west of Bainbridge Island to visit the little town in Liberty Bay called Poulsbo, which calls itself the "Little Norway on the Fjord."

I was greeted by the sound of a band concert as I tied the boat to the town's large public dock. Children played on the steps of a white pavilion, and picnickers sprawled on the grass under shaded trees. I walked across the park to the open doors of a repair garage. Inside, tires, jacks, generators, engine blocks and greasy auto parts had been shoved to one side to make room for the town's shirt-sleeved band rehearsing for a concert.

The young conductor was working the musicians through just the right feeling for a crescendo that climaxed the marching tune they were playing. In pauses, they reached under their chairs to bring out cans of beer for a quick sip between measures. There was no room in the garage for a sit-down audience, but appreciative spectators stood outside, tapping their feet in time with the music.

Poulsbo has turned its ethnic Scandinavian history into an artistic, architectural and cultural theme that is a tourist draw for thousands of summer visitors. On the main street, among numerous art galleries, gift and antique shops, there is Tivoli Place, Nordic House, the Verksted Gallery and a store advertising "Old World Viking Ice Creme Cones." At one end of the town, a mural pictures a flaxen-haired young couple standing arm in arm by a creek, gazing together at distant mountain peaks. Below the mural, a timbered replica of a clock tower keeps no time but serves as a prominent place for a large sign reading "Velkommen to Poulsbo." The largest building in town is the Sons of Norway Hall. A side door led me to the Troll Room, and overhead, tromping feet kept time to an accordion tune as the sons and daughters of Norway danced a brisk polka. In the waterfront park stands a bronze statue of a bearded Viking. Off to the southeast looms Mount Rainier; to the west, the jagged skyline of the Olympics stands above timbered slopes of black-green hills, a view that must have looked to those people who settled here much like their distant Norwegian homeland.

I didn't try to make sense out of Poulsbo. I was just a tourist there among many: snapping pictures, window shopping and eating Old World Ice Creme Cones. The next morning, at dawn, the open hatch above my bunk was a pale square of light in the roof of my bedroom. Some clock within awoke me to the half-light of the morning and I got up to stand in the hatch. Seagulls circled around the boat in silent spirals. Far to the southeast, an invisible sun washed the summit of Mount Rainier with a pink light. My housekeeping chores were finished in minutes: sleeping bag rolled up, pillow stuffed under the bunk, last night's book returned to the shelf and the dregs of the morning coffee sloshed over the side. I was ready for the day, and I headed north to catch up with two sailing ships anchored just off Elliot Point in Possession Sound.

On May 31, the *Discovery* and the *Chatham* had sailed into Possession Sound, which opens to some complicated passages lying to the east of Whidbey Island. Their course along the mainland carried them into the inlet of Port Susan, where the *Chatham* ran aground in the shallows north of Kayak Point. It was refloated on the flood tide without damage. The leadsman, who had reported incorrect soundings, was blamed for the grounding and punished with 36 lashes.

Whidbey, meanwhile, was off exploring Saratoga Passage and the shoreline of the island Vancouver would later name in his honour. At Hope Island in the upper part of Skagit Bay, Whidbey turned around, believing that he had reached the end of the passage. And so he had, but by not going farther, he had missed the hard left turn just ahead at the northern end of Whidbey Island that leads to Deception Pass.

In my boat, I followed Whidbey's track up to the northern end of Skagit Bay and from there I could see how he had made this oversight. The channel between Hope Island and Ala Spit on Whidbey Island becomes very narrow. The view through the channel is further blocked by Skagit Island and, beyond that, the shoreline of Fidalgo Island. Anyone unfamiliar with the area or without a chart would have no reason to suspect that the channel here would make an abrupt turn that would lead to an unseen pass, later given the appropriate name Deception Pass by Vancouver.

There is a sign on the highway bridge crossing Deception Pass that tells of Vancouver naming the pass on his 1792 expedition. Until I read that sign, I had had no idea that such a voyage had ever happened, but the idea of it fascinated me and led to my later interest in the Vancouver expedition.

Other names left behind in the area of Possession Sound by Vancouver were Penn Cove for Granville Penn, Port Susan for Lady Susanna Gardner and Port Gardner for Captain Allen Gardner, who recommended Vancouver for command of his expedition. Vancouver was particularly impressed with the area around Penn Cove, writing that it

> ... presented a delightful prospect, consisting chiefly of
> spacious meadows, elegantly adorned with clumps of

trees; amongst which the oak bore a very considerable proportion, in size from four to six feet in circumference. In these beautiful pastures, bordering on an expansive sheet of water, the deer were seen playing about in great numbers. Nature had here provided the well-stocked park, and wanted only the assistance of art to constitute that desirable assemblage of surface, which is so much sought in other countries ... The soil principally consisted of a rich, black vegetable mould, lying on a sandy or clayey substratum; the grass, of an excellent quality, grew to the height of three feet, and the ferns, which, in the sandy soils, occupied the clear spots, were nearly twice as high.

Sunday, June 4, was declared a holiday aboard the two ships to honour the birthday of King George III, England's reigning monarch. To celebrate, the crew was served a special dinner and a double ration of grog to drink to His Majesty's health. On this day, at the point of land he named Possession Point at the southern end of Whidbey Island, Vancouver, with his officers and some crew members, landed to formally take possession in the king's name of the waters and shores surrounding what Vancouver named the Gulf of Georgia.

There must have been a few people watching from the 425-foot white bluff of Possession Point. What they were about to witness, in this probable scene, would forever change their lives, because their land, their sea, their home would no longer be theirs alone after this day. Across from where they were watching, two ships were anchored just off the shore, their sails tightly furled, yards crossed, the black snouts of cannons projecting through raised ports. Toward the shore, in measured strokes, came boats manned by bearded sailors wearing tarred hats and striped shirts. On the seats between the rowers sat rigid marines holding their sky-pointing bayoneted rifles. In the stern sat crimson-clad officers and behind them waved a gigantic flag, showing the brilliantly coloured crossbars of the Union Jack.

The boats landed and the sailors leaped out to haul them up the beach. The marines, in uniforms girded with freshly clayed white cross belts, formed up in a double line. Between them, with slow-stepped dignity, the officers walked to the top of the beach. Hats were removed; the shaft of the flag was pushed into the sand. In a circle around the flag, all listened to one in the centre, more splendid than the others in his uniform of white pants and brass-buttoned red coat. When he stopped speaking, the sound of cheering rising up from the beach was drowned by the booming salvo of cannons from the ships.

With this ceremony below the bluff, Vancouver took "formal possession of all the countries we had lately been employed in exploring in the name of and for His Britannic Majesty, [and] his heirs." The Mediterranean of the North was now an English sea, named for a king who, in a few years, would wander his palace halls in darkness and dementia.

Vancouver defined the water and land he had claimed for his king by latitude and longitude, a system of grid lines imposed on the earth that also enclosed the people who, for thousands of years, had lived on that land and by that sea. They knew that area only by the curved lines of its shores, the ringed beaches of islands and the twisting turns of bays and inlets. "Place" was defined by where the fishing was good, where shellfish grew in abundance, where salmon returned from the sea to fight their way up a river.

Now and forever, the geography of their curving world would be contained within lines that referred to time and celestial bodies:

latitude and longitude. Latitude they probably would have understood because it related to the sun and stars, which occupied different positions throughout the day and the year and which had, in turn, a bearing on the changing hours of daylight and the changing seasons of the year. Longitude, a measure of time, would have been beyond their comprehension because they measured time by the rise and fall of the tides, the spawn of the herring, the birth of a child, the death of a chief. But then, what use was that grid system for defining location if one knew where he had come from and where he was going along routes and way signs that had been followed for thousands of years and hundreds of generations?

At Possession Point, then, the confrontation of two cultures. One, the "primitive" culture of an indigenous people, and the other, a culture based on the philosophy of the Age of Enlightenment, that liberal, humanitarian movement of the 18th century that offered a scientific and rational approach to political and social issues. The Vancouver expedition, with its compassionate and non-judgmental intercourse with First Nations, the condition of order and good health maintained aboard the ships, its collections and studies of indigenous plants and animals, its scientific perspective and its non-commercial objectives, was a model of this philosophy.

The apotheosis of the Enlightenment era were James Cook's three voyages to the Pacific, 1768 to 1780. These were the first to have as their sole objective geographic and scientific exploration, with the first voyage an outstanding example of this mindset. It was staffed with naturalists and artists who worked under the direction of Joseph Banks, the esteemed British naturalist who for years served as president of the Royal Society. One of the scientific objectives of this first voyage was the placement of an observatory on the island of Tahiti to observe the transit of Venus across the face of the sun as part of an international effort to measure the distance between the earth and the sun. (The calculated distance of 153,000,000 kilometres determined was just over the 149,604,970 kilometres accepted today.) Vancouver did not sail on this first voyage, but he inherited Cook's enlightened views when he sailed with him on his other two voyages.

One aspect of this era was the improvement in the food the British navy served to its sailors in an effort to reduce scurvy. Cook, the most enlightened seaman of his age, had stocked his ship with sauerkraut, dried meat and vegetable soup mixes, and gathered fresh fruit and vegetables whenever they were available along the routes of his voyages. He was absolutely rigid in demanding that his crew eat this unwelcome food and a few men who refused were punished with the lash. As a result, he was able to sail his three voyages of over 160,000 miles with very few outbreaks of scurvy.

In spite of the stereotype of the underfed British sailor, writes N. A. Rogers, "the diet supplied by the establishment was plain and very restricted in its range, but it provided more than sufficient calories for hard physical work." The poor of England during the latter part of the 18th century were often underfed, he points out. The sailors' food, by contrast, was good and plentiful and the seaman, comments Rogers, "who had a hot dinner daily, with beef and beer, bread and cheese, and sometimes vegetables and fruit, was eating well by his standards."

He lists the standard naval issue of food for one man for a week in the Georgian navy: seven pounds of bread, seven gallons of beer, four pounds of beef, one quart of peas, three pints of oatmeal, six ounces of butter and twelve ounces of cheese.

Cleanliness was another advance of this era and the navy's efforts to keep its ships clean were impressive. The pathology of the time believed that disease was carried by "bad air" that would arise from the fetid stinks of a ship's hold and from the closeness of men sleeping and working in crowded conditions. The airing of bedding and the washing of clothing were enforced measures of cleanliness whenever weather permitted. To rid the ship of noxious orders, gunpowder was burned below the decks and they were then washed down with warm vinegar.

For mariners like Cook and Vancouver, the great achievement of the age was the new science of navigation based on time, a totally new method made possible by a clock that could maintain accuracy at sea. Such a clock had been invented by an English watchmaker, John Harrison. Down through the ages, mariners had been able to find their latitude by the simple observation of the sun's angle above the equator. Finding longitude, however, was a matter of guesswork. With an accurate clock (chronometer), a navigator was able to compare his sea time with the time in some fixed location, primarily Greenwich Mean Time in England. The time difference between the two locations could then be converted to the degrees of separation between the two points. Vancouver commented on this advance in the science of navigation:

> By the introduction of nautical astronomy into marine education ... it is now become evident, that sea officers of the most common-rate abilities, who will take the trouble of making themselves acquainted with the principles of this science, will, on all suitable occasions, with proper and correct instruments, be enabled to acquire a knowledge of their situation in the Atlantic, Indian, or Pacific Oceans, with a degree of accuracy sufficient to steer ... to any known spot.

Inevitable, then, was the aftermath of what took place at Possession Point. One culture was locked into its past, another culture was expressing a new philosophy that, in time, would lead first to the industrial age, then the scientific age and lastly — and almost too late — an emerging humanistic and political concern for all the peoples of the Inland Sea. Their lives were forever changed after that event on the morning of June 4, 1792, at Possession Point.

Before departing from Possession Point, Vancouver bestowed the name "Admiralty Inlet" on the waters so far explored with the exception of the most southerly lower area of Puget Sound. In his mind, the body of water from Port Townsend to present-day Tacoma was to carry this name. On today's charts, a much smaller Admiralty Inlet begins at Port Townsend and concludes at Point No Point across from Whidbey Island's Useless Bay. I enjoyed sailing through Admiralty Inlet, holding tight to the margins of its shores to steer clear of the many ships heading south for the ports of Seattle, Tacoma and Olympia or outward bound to the Pacific. For me, the name itself, "Admiralty," recalled images of a mutton-chopped old sea dog, resplendent in stiff, gold-striped cuffs, black tie and saltwater-stained cap.

June 5 saw the ships sailing down Possession Sound in pleasant weather. There was a peaceful scene on the *Discovery*'s deck on that June morning described by Vancouver:

> Whilst we were passing gently on, the [Indian] chief, who had shewn so much friendly attention to Mr. Whidbey and his party, with several of his friends came on board, and presented us with some fruit and dried fish. He entered the ship with some reluctance, but was no sooner on deck than he seemed perfectly reconciled; and with much inquisitive earnestness regarded the surrounding objects, the novelty of which seem to fill his mind with surprise and admiration ...

> After he had visited the different parts of the ship, at
> which he expressed the greatest astonishment, I pre-
> sented him and his friends with an assortment of such
> things as they esteemed to be most valuable; and then
> they took their leave, seemingly highly pleased with
> their reception.

With the wind failing, the *Discovery* anchored off the western shore of Admiralty Inlet, halfway between Oak Bay and Marrowstone Point, the *Chatham* just astern. The wind remained light and on the next day the two ships came to anchor off Partridge Point on Whidbey Island (Vancouver's brother, John, had married a Martha Partridge). A lack of wind held the ships in this position until June 7. While waiting, Vancouver and Broughton went to Smith Island in the pinnace with sextants to verify the locations of Point Wilson (named for Captain George Wilson, Royal Navy) and Protection Island.

Had Vancouver been able to see over the horizon and out to Cape Flattery that day, he would have seen two Spanish ships, the *Sutil* and the *Mexicana*, entering the Strait of Juan de Fuca. The meeting between Vancouver and the two Spanish captains, Dionisio Alcalá Galiano and Cayetano Valdés, would occur later.

On June 8, the course north was resumed with the *Discovery* sailing up Rosario Strait, past Lopez, Decatur and Blakely islands and coming to anchor in Strawberry Bay on Cypress Island. (Broughton had found strawberries on the island while exploring the San Juans; what Vancouver called cypress were native junipers.) Later, the *Chatham* arrived in the bay. Lack of wind forced a layover for another day and Broughton and Menzies were able to make a short exploration of the eastern San Juan Islands. Menzies wrote this description of the islands which, more than two centuries later,

would still be an accurate description: "The land rose rugged &
hilly to a moderate height & was composed of massive solid Rocks
covered with a thin layer of blackish mould which offered nourish-
ment to a straddling forest of small stunted pines. The Shores were
almost every where steep & cliffy which made Landing difficult &
the woods were in many places equally difficult of access from the
rocky cliffs & chasms with which they abounded."

Puget and Whidbey in the launch and cutter were sent out with
a week's supply of provisions to survey the unexplored eastern
mainland shore, and on this voyage they discovered the inlet of
Deception Pass separating Whidbey and Fidalgo islands, which
Broughton had missed. The pass was described as "a very narrow
and intricate channel, which, for a considerable distance, was not
forty yards in width, and abounded with rocks ... in addition to the
great rapidity and irregularity of the tide."

Puget and Whidbey did not attempt to enter Deception Pass
but continued their exploration north around Fidalgo Point and
through Guemes Channel to explore Padilla Bay. From there, the
view opened northward to Bellingham Bay (honouring Sir William
Bellingham) and the open horizon of the Strait of Georgia.

On June 11, the two ships sailed up Rosario Strait between Orcas
and Lummi islands, entered the lower end of the Strait of Georgia,
and anchored in the harbour Vancouver named Birch Bay because
of the stands of black birch growing there.

I felt the excitement of open water as I sailed into the immense,
20-mile-wide opening of the Strait of Georgia that seemed to

stretch northwestward without end. This is speculation on my part, but I think there might also have been a sense of excitement aboard the *Discovery* as it sailed into this wide strait, as it could have been the opening to a northwest passage. I base this speculation on a statement made by Lieutenant Broughton during his survey of the San Juans; he believed a channel north from the islands "communicated with what we call'd the true NW passage." If Vancouver and his men thought they had happened upon that rumoured "true" passage, their excitement would indeed have been apparent.

An observatory was established on the shore of Birch Bay for checking the accuracy of the chronometers. Whidbey was instructed to take the *Discovery*'s cutter south to explore the mainland shore and Bellingham Bay, passed on the voyage north.

Then, wrote Vancouver, "Matters thus arranged, with a week's provision in each boat, I departed at five o'clock in the morning of Tuesday, the 12th." Vancouver took the launch, Puget the pinnace, and together they started out on what was to be a remarkable 11-day, 350-mile voyage along the mainland shore of the Strait of Georgia. I looked forward to following this boat voyage, but before doing so I wanted to visit the Canadian Gulf Islands looming just across the strait.

The Gulf Islands

BEFORE I EVER LANDED ON AN ISLAND, I WAS EXPLORING THEM. Those explorations were made across the top of my fourth-grade wooden desk. No one looking at the desk would know that the peculiar pattern of dots and scratches I made with a pencil point across its top was my secret chart of the South Seas. The dots stood for islands, the scratches imagined voyages I sailed through those seas.

"Stand by the braces, ready about and helms alee," were the inaudible commands I issued to drown out the drone of the class-room recitations around me. The ship under my command beat around the island archipelago of the ink well, avoided the reef of the pencil grove and set a course WSW with the trades to Tahiti, a thousand leagues away in the upper left-hand corner of the desk. I learned arithmetic by projecting compass courses across the desk to island destinations of latitude and longitude; history and geography from reading books by James Cook, Herman Melville, Joseph Conrad, Robert Louis Stevenson and Jack London. All of this played out on that desktop chart, voyages of adventures that carried me away from the dull and dreary fourth-grade classroom, out the window and across the sea to those distant islands lying just below the horizon.

And today, many years later, islands still have a special hold on my romantic imagination. An island, I believe, is more than that terse dictionary definition of a land mass surrounded by water. This description leaves out the unique character that I think defines an island: a place that lies outside and beyond the confines of ordinary life, a place where time is tied to the immutable laws of the winds, seasons and tides. Throughout Western literature, islands have served as settings for adventure, noble deeds and skullduggery. Defoe, Twain, Melville, Stevenson, London, Maugham, Michener, Durrell — all of these authors placed some of their most colourful characters and exciting stories in island settings, there to deal in isolation and insularity with themes and stories that touch on all the emotions, dreams and ambitions of human life.

And right over my bow, as I entered the Gulf Island chain, was just such an island: D'Arcy, the most southerly island in the group. The island today is a provincial marine park, a lovely place of narrow beaches backed by madroña and pine trees that belies D'Arcy's dark history as described by Dr. Ernest Hall, who visited the island in 1891. He wrote:

About a league off the eastern coast of Vancouver Island ... lies the pretty little island of D'Arcy. Viewed from the deck of a vessel as she ploughs her way seaward, it presents a delightful picture to the eye. Almost its entire surface is covered with a dense growth of pine, cedar and spruce. This bank of verdure extends to the edge of the pebble beach, where at high tide the waters of the Pacific kiss and caress the feet of the forest monarchs, whose verdant crowns stand out in bold relief against the milder tints of sea and sky. Although the gem of the East Coast Islands, the shores of D'Arcy Island are rarely pressed by the feet of the white man, and few indeed are the prows which grate upon its beach. Travelers in these waters dread the storm which forces them upon its coast even for a night and the superstitious Siwash trolling for salmon pulls with a swifter oar as he discerns ahead the outline of her shores. For hidden away yonder in their little cabins under the grateful shade of the fir with their hot blood burning out their lives, the victims of this plague are slowly dying with their faces to the rising sun.

The plague was leprosy, and Dr. Hall had come to D'Arcy to inspect the leper colony established there in 1891. Earlier in that year, five Chinese people working in Victoria were diagnosed with leprosy. Panicked by the fear of the disease spreading, the city council of Victoria acquired D'Arcy, and those five men were taken to the island to live there in isolation and pain until they died.

There were thousands of Chinese workers throughout British Columbia at the time, brought there to work the mines and build railroads. Whenever one of them was afflicted with the dread disease, he was banished to the island. There, the leper colony consisted of a line of huts huddling under a common roof. Supplies — food, whiskey, opium and coffins — were taken to the island only four times a year. Isolation, not treatment, was how leprosy was handled there in those years. The inmates on D'Arcy languished in the most primitive conditions as various governmental agencies argued about which one should bear the cost of the colony. None wanted to, at least at a level that might have improved living conditions for the lepers of D'Arcy. In 1907, the problem was solved by giving each survivor $300 and passage on a tramp steamer back to China. The next year a federal report on D'Arcy concluded by stating, "All cabins burned."

The largest Gulf Island, Saltspring, was one of the earliest islands to be settled. In 1859, a group of down-and-out Australian land-seekers bought land on the island for a shilling an acre. The early years of the island were filled with the usual problems and conflicts of pioneer settlements. Indian raids were frequent, farm animals fell prey to wolves and cougars, freight service was spasmodic and provisions were often in short supply. But grit and determination prevailed, orchards were planted, sheep introduced to the island, a school and church were built and, by 1895, the population had grown to 450 residents.

As I walked the streets of Ganges, the island's main village, looking at art galleries, restaurants, pubs, trinket shops, clothing stores and real estate offices offering homes in the six-figure range, my thoughts switched from history to questions about the island's future.

Today, Saltspring Island — like all the Gulf Islands — confronts the problems of too many people and too much development. Everything about the islands is just too nice: scenery, water-related pleasures, mild weather, modest rainfall, a good cultural environment and accessibility to the metropolitan cites of Victoria and Vancouver. The area around the Strait of Georgia is densely populated, and, the number of people there is expected to double in the next 25 years. It is a future that brings residents of the islands to their knees with a prayer:

> O Lord we thank Thee that by thy grace
> Thou has brought us to this lovely place.
> But now, O Lord, we humbly pray:
> Thou shalt keep all others away.

"What's to become of the islands?" I asked a young staff member of the Islands Trust office in Ganges. Her answers covered the kinds of problems found wherever population and development pressures are pitted against the interests of conservation, wildlife and scenic resources.

But there is some hope. The Islands Trust is dedicated to preserve and protect some aspects of the islands and their special environments. On one island within the Trust, she explained, an absolute limit had been placed on the number of houses that could be built.

"Is the Trust doing a good job?" I asked her.

"I think so," she answered.

"How can you tell?"

"Because," she replied, "half the people hate us and the other half love us."

In Ganges, there are many efforts on the part of island people, government agencies and environmental groups to prevent the islands from becoming a paradise lost. They work from a variety of viewpoints, some co-operative, many in conflict, hoping to hold the line on population increases, logging, and urban and rural development. But the human footprints and tire tracks are everywhere invasive, tending to erode those qualities that define the special essence and appeal of an island. Much of what the islanders sought to avoid by coming here has spilled over from the mainland: traffic, shopping centres, parking lots, huge homes, tourists and more and more "private, keep out" signs posted by off-island homeowners.

It is not my task or privilege to criticize how the islanders run their island, but as a visitor, I have some right to hope that something can be done to lessen the outside world's impact. A right that says that they own the land, but not the exclusive right to the universal symbol of an island. Unfortunately, that symbol — whatever its various meanings to various people — has become a commercial, saleable product, promoted by the magazine ads of travel agencies, airlines and cruise ships. While waiting for a haircut in Ganges, I thumbed through a few such publications. One calls itself just *Islands*.

Inside the magazine are colourful ads, each targeted to the theme of enjoying an island experience. One was a hotel ad showing photos of exotic drinks, barefoot beach walkers and a sunset over a palm-studded beach with the copy reading: "Everyone wants to be here. Don't you?" I had to wonder what land-bound copywriter came up with this line: "Saltwater lingering on lips after snorkeling in a crystal cove." And lastly, an ad with the picture of a well-tanned man and woman leaping hand in hand through the surf with the claim that "at our resorts, you'll feel a strong temptation to get in touch with your inner child. To run on the beach. To play all day and still want more." *More?* What more could there possibly be?

In defence of my visit to Saltspring Island as one more tourist among thousands, I at least had the argument that I had come by boat and that, in itself, fulfils another island definition — a bit of land surrounded by the need of a boat.

The history of the Gulf Islands is the story of those who came to these islands because they were escaping the law, stranded between grandiose projects that did not pan out or settling there simply because the land was open, the sea breezes fresh and the opportunities promising.

The first white settlers on the Gulf Islands were former employees of the Hudson's Bay Company and miners returning broke from the Fraser and Cariboo gold fields of the 1860s. Many were expatriates from Great Britain, some poor, but others from the upper classes and even aristocratic members of English society who sold the old manse and took up residence in the islands, bringing with them their silver, furniture, heirlooms, paintings and tea cozies.

Three of them — long gone — I would like to have met, so I sailed over from Saltspring to the outer Gulf Islands and tied up at the little community on Mayne Island. Georgina Point forms the northeast tip of Mayne Island, a magnificent site that overlooks tide-ripped Active Pass and the open waters of the Strait of Georgia. Until a few years ago, the old Point Comfort Hotel stood on that point and the three people I would like to have known were associated with that hotel.

One was the man who built the three-storey, 35-room hotel: Warburton Pike, one of the more colourful Gulf Island characters. English born and an Oxford graduate, he had been an Arctic explorer, a cowboy, a prairie hunter and a gold miner before coming to the Gulf Islands in 1884. He was most at home in the bush and preferred to sleep under a tree in the front yard of his home on Saturna Island instead of in his bedroom. He had the odd and disquieting habit of going off by himself from time to time on extended forays into the bush or up-island in his sailboat.

Warburton Pike. The name suggests someone larger than life, and so he was: over six feet tall, heavily built, moustached, roughly dressed in clothes of good wool, a curved pipe always in his mouth. He returned to England in 1914 to enlist in the army, but, rejected in trying to fulfil his duty to queen and country, he became depressed and committed suicide. I rather thought that Mr. Pike would have made a good sailing companion aboard *Kea*, except that, because of his height, he would not have been able to stand up in the cabin or sleep in one of its bunks.

Point Comfort carried on as a hotel until it was purchased by a teetotalling family that, in closing the bar, lost the hotel's chief source of income. It was later purchased by two other island characters I would like to have met: Colonel and Lady Fawkes, who sold their ancient mansion in Bedhampton, England, and — with their very British ways — came to live on Mayne Island.

Their arrival by boat must have caused a bit of a stir. The colonel stepped ashore wearing a suit, tie and straw hat. His leather water bottle hung from one shoulder, his canvas bag with sketching pad and paints was slung over the other, and in his hand, he carried his easel. Behind him came Lady Constance, wearing gumboots and a full-length gown and coat, both chewed at the hemline by her pet dog.

In 1924 they purchased the run-down hotel and renamed it Culzean for Lady Constance's ancestral home in Scotland. Cold baths were a daily ritual of the household, as were summer tennis and croquet matches with tea served on the lawn. The colonel sketched and his lady worked on her loom, sewing underwear for the poor children of Vancouver. On boat days, she carried her portable organ to the dock and greeted incoming passengers with hymns.

Colonel Fawkes died at Culzean in 1931, Lady Constance in 1946. She willed Culzean, crates of unpacked furniture, 10 tons of household furnishings and 400 of the colonel's paintings to their caretaker. Taxes on the estate, however, forced him to sell it in 1946 for $13,000. The hotel was demolished in 1958.

From Mayne Island, I sailed up Trincomali Channel, then over to Vancouver Island to visit the town of Chemainus, which advertises itself as "The Mural Capital of North America and the World." Half a million people a year come to visit this little town that painted itself to prosperity and international recognition by covering its downtown buildings with murals that tell in vivid colours the history of the area.

In 1983, the mill, which had sustained the town for 120 years, closed and Chemainus faced economic disaster. Before the mill's closure, town leaders had initiated a downtown redevelopment plan and, on the basis of this civic energy, the Festival of Murals Association was organized to turn the downtown into the world's largest outdoor art gallery. A quarter of a million dollars was invested in the mural project, which by 1992 boasted 32 murals and six sculptures, all created by internationally known artists.

I walked the streets on a Sunday morning and it seemed that every corner was staffed by a friendly volunteer most anxious to talk about and boast about what their little community had accomplished. On the outskirts of the town, I saw what appeared to be a huge gateway and, behind, it just an empty field.

"Why such a huge entry gate to a vacant lot?" I asked one of the volunteers.

"We built that huge gate to give an idea of what we plan to build in that field. Someday, it will contain artists and workshops from all nations of the Pacific working together here to produce their native art and crafts."

From Chemainus, I travelled up through Stuart Channel and went through Dodd Narrows on a slack tide to Nanaimo. A Sunday breakfast was what I was hungry for as I tied up at the port dock. It was still early when I found a hotel dining room where a young hostess seated me. Before me was a white tablecloth and starched napkins, folded into little wings that fanned out from crystal goblets.

I ordered breakfast, then went to the men's room to wash. It was scented with rose petals in oyster-shell dishes on the counter. After three weeks of peeing in a coffee can on the boat, I found it somehow amusing to pee in the elaborate, white-enamelled, constantly flushing urinal with its little lemon-smelling pink disk at the centre of its swirling water.

The hotel guests had wandered in when I returned to the dining room. They smelled sweetly of shower soap, perfume and shaving lotion. My toast arrived, standing on edge in a little silver cage with encircling tiny plastic cubes of jelly. I nearly gagged on the spread of bacon, eggs and hash browns the waitress placed on my table. For too long, I had been accustomed to a swallow of rum, a handful of raisins and a bowl of granola for breakfast. I left the hotel, the breakfast half-eaten, and walked along Nanaimo's seaside esplanade where flags snapped in the wind and water taxis carried happy groups of Sunday picnickers across the harbour to Newcastle Island.

All of this, I reflected, was a far different city from the old coal-mining settlement founded by the Hudson's Bay Company in the 1850s. Steamships were then beginning to replace sailing ships, and shipping coal from Wales to British Columbia to supply the Royal Navy squadron at Esquimalt was very expensive. The California gold rush had opened a huge market for coal, so when a Salish Indian chief delivered a canoe-load of coal he had dug at Nanaimo to a Fort Victoria blacksmith, the company established mining operations there.

By 1855, Nanaimo was a settlement of 42 houses with a European population of 150, mostly miners brought over from Wales and Scotland. When the company sold its mines to the Vancouver Coal and Land Company, Nanaimo became — for a while — a kind of industrial utopia. The company had an enlightened management philosophy, believing that company profits were directly related to worker satisfaction. Every miner was given a house and a garden plot; the company donated land for a park and sponsored sports and cultural events. The 170 widows of a disastrous mine explosion were given lifetime free rent and fuel.

By the turn of the century, the city's population reached 10,000, 2,000 of whom were employed in the mines. But the industrial peace of Nanaimo was about to be shattered by an American import: the revolutionary International Workers of the World, known as "Wobblies." The organization gained many supporters from among the ranks of the immigrant coal workers and, in 1913, a thousand striking miners took possession of Nanaimo; they burned and looted buildings and shot a strikebreaker and a police officer. A regiment of militia was dispatched from Victoria to put down the riot. More than 50 of the strikers were given severe prison sentences and the militia occupied Nanaimo for a year to prevent further outbreaks.

The major industry today in Nanaimo is the huge pulp and paper mill south of the city. That and its large commercial fishing fleet and a diminishing number of lumber mills provide the workforce that historically has dominated the city.

Nanaimo is still gritty enough to be called a blue-collar working town, but it is a textbook study in the transition of a city from yesterday to today as it seeks to develop a new urban profile. Like Port Townsend, that new profile will be based on history and Nanaimo's waterfront, now ringed with a landscaped esplanade and the curving row of upscale condominiums. I hope, however, that as these new developments spread, something of that old grit will remain in Nanaimo as an antidote to the creeping sameness that is the character of so many cities today.

I left Nanaimo, made a fast downwind sail back through the long chain of the Gulf Islands and then crossed the Strait of Georgia to follow Vancouver as he set out in two ship's boats from Birch Bay to explore the mainland shore of the strait.

Through the Strait of Georgia

TO ANSWER A PERPLEXING QUESTION, I FOLLOWED THE EXACT course taken by Vancouver and Puget as they left Birch Bay and travelled up the Strait of Georgia. The question was why or how did Vancouver miss seeing the mouth of the Fraser River, the largest river along the British Columbia coast?

The two boats reached Point Roberts by noon and then their course was turned away from the mainland by the shallows of Roberts Bank (both named for a Captain Henry Roberts who sailed with Cook). Vancouver wrote:

> We proceeded, but soon found our progress along
> the eastern or continental shore materially impeded
> by a shoal that extends from Point Roberts ... seven
> or eight miles, then stretches NW about five or six

miles further, where it takes a northerly direction ...
Along the edge of this bank we had soundings from
ten to one fathom, as we increased or decreased our
distance from the eastern shore; to approach which
all our endeavors were exerted to no purpose, until
nine in the evening, when the shoal having forced us
nearly into the middle of the gulf, we stood over to its
western side, in order to land for the night ... As we
stood to the westward, our depth soon increased to
15 fathoms, after which we gained no bottom until we
reached the western shore of the gulf, where, on our
arrival about one o' clock in the morning, it was with
much difficulty we were enabled to land on the steep
rugged rocks that compose the coast, for the purpose
of cooking only, and were compelled to remain and
sleep in the boats.

This — an open boat on the rocky shore of Galiano Island — was
their place of rest after 20 hours of rowing and sailing. The next
day, June 13, the boats were underway at 5:00 a.m. and by noon
they reached Point Grey. (Captain George Grey was a friend of
Vancouver.) It was on this day's voyage that Vancouver passed the
Fraser without recognizing it as a major river. His journal describes
what he saw:

... a very low land, apparently a swampy flat, that
retires several miles, before the country rises to meet
the rugged snowy mountains, which we found still
continuing in a direction nearly along the coast. This
low flat being very much inundated ... gives its high
land, when seen at a distance, the appearance of an

island; this, however, is not the case, notwithstanding there are two openings between this point and Point Grey. These can only be navigable for canoes, as the shoal continues along the coast to the distance of seven or eight miles from the shore, on which were lodged, and especially before these openings, logs of wood, and stumps of trees innumerable.

Vancouver was seeing two of the three outlets of the Fraser River without realizing they were the mouths of this great river, and for this he has been criticized. In my boat, I followed his track — not to excuse him for missing the river, but to understand why. The configuration of Roberts Bank, I think, offers the explanation.

Roberts Bank today extends five miles out into the Strait of Georgia. Vancouver, as he passed the bank, estimated it to be seven to eight miles wide. Accepting his estimate, I travelled up the strait his estimated eight miles off the shore. From my height, standing in the boat, my visible horizon was only 2.8 nautical miles, as it would have been for Vancouver standing in his boat. I could see nothing of the low mainland shore, and, by ignoring the obvious channel markers, nothing to my eye suggested the outflow of a major river. But those logs and stumps Vancouver did see should have suggested that they had been carried there by a sizable outflow from some large river. But perhaps not, because in his time — as well as today — stumps and tree trunks are a common sight along the shores.

There is another possible reason for his oversight. My reading of Vancouver's journal leads me to believe that he was not expecting to find a major river along this shore because he saw the coast continually backed by the unbroken line of the Cascades and other mountain ranges. Some 15 of his previous log entries referred to the height and alignment north and south of this range "to connect the whole in one barrier along the coast." From Point Roberts, just south of the Fraser, he again observed a line of "rugged snowy mountains which we found still continuing in a direction nearly along the coast." Thus, it is possible that Vancouver set out from Birch Bay without any geographical evidence to suggest the chain was broken by any river of importance. Out there off that shallow bank I saw what Vancouver saw: nothing that looked like a river.

The Fraser has an immense effect on the Strait of Georgia, draining an area of 230,000 square kilometres. Along its 1,370-kilometre journey from the west slope of the Rocky Mountains, the river picks up thousands of feeder streams to accumulate an outflow of water at its mouth that can measure in hundreds of thousands of cubic feet per day in the high-water months of June and July. The Fraser River estuary, 37 kilometres wide between Point Roberts and Point Grey, is the largest such opening on the B.C. coast. Tides affect the river as far as Chilliwack, 120 kilometres inland from the river's mouth.

The river's outflow, along with its burden of silt, fans out in the shape of a large plume when it mixes with the waters of the Strait of Georgia. The line between the plume and the seawater is very distinct: clear on one side, the other side murky in various shades of grey. Because fresh water is lighter than salt water, the Fraser plume is a huge plane of fresh water from one to ten metres deep floating in a sea of salt. (That distinct line, of course, is something else Vancouver should have noticed as evidence of the outfall of a large river.)

The Fraser remained an unknown river until 1793 when Alexander Mackenzie, a partner in the North West Company, found its headwaters and followed the river until it became too dangerous for canoe travel. He then crossed overland and reached tidewater at the mouth of the Bella Coola River. His was the first expedition to cross North America, 12 years before Lewis and Clark. At the mouth of the Bella Coola, he inscribed his memorial with a mixture of grease and vermilion. It read "Alex Mackenzie from Canada by land 22 July 1793." Neither time nor vandals have destroyed his painted letters and they can still be clearly read today.

The river is named for Simon Fraser, another partner in the North West Company, who came down the Fraser in 1808, believing it to be the Columbia. The journey carried him to the mouth of the river and the disappointing conclusion that the river was too dangerous to provide a trade route from the company's interior forts to the sea.

Vancouver's two boats came in from the strait, rounded Point Grey and headed eastward up Burrard Inlet past present-day Vancouver. (Sir Henry Burrard had sailed with Vancouver in the West Indies.) Here, in a flight of fantasy, I wished I could have said, "Right over there, Captain Vancouver, a city will be founded in 94 years and named for you and in that city today there are over 500 commercial firms bearing your name."

The city's Stanley Park was then an island that the boats sailed around. Beyond the First Narrows, Vancouver was welcomed by a group of 50 Natives who gave him a present of cooked fish. The exploration of Burrard Inlet then took the boats to Port Moody and a rocky campsite on the south shore opposite Indian Arm. That night, most of the men slept in the boats, though a few slept on the narrow beach, only to be flooded by the high tide. The boats cleared Burrard Inlet on the morning of June 14 heading for the point Vancouver named Point Atkinson for a "particular friend."

I lived in Vancouver for a brief time and from my apartment window I could see the distant outline of Point Atkinson. Whenever I looked at that point, I thought of it as a portal to the unknown that lay beyond. Now, two ships were leading me into that unknown, as they rounded Point Atkinson and entered Howe Sound.

Howe Sound introduced the men of the expedition (and me) to a different dimension of geography: the deep, ice-carved fjords of the mainland British Columbia coast. As the men worked their way up the coast, each long inlet would present them with the daunting ordeal of exploring it, because any one of them might have been the entrance to that sought-for water passage across the continent.

The name Passage Island was given to a small island in the opening to Howe Sound, Anvil Island to another because it is shaped like an anvil. The boats were driven up the sound by a "fresh southerly gale attended with dark gloomy weather, that greatly added to the dreary prospect of the surrounding country," wrote Vancouver. He described the sound:

> The low fertile shores we had been accustomed to see ... here no longer existed; their place was now occupied by the base of the stupendous snowy barrier, thinly wooded and rising from the sea abruptly to the clouds; from whose frigid summit, the dissolving snow in foaming torrents rushed down the sides of chasms of its rugged surface, exhibiting altogether a sublime, though gloomy spectacle, which animated nature seem to have deserted. Not a bird, nor living creature

was to be seen, and the roaring of the falling cataracts
in every direction precluded their being heard, had
any been in our neighbourhood.

Howe Sound, a "gloomy spectacle" for Vancouver, was for me
a place of magnificent and overpowering scenery as I sailed its
length, but then, I was not driven up the sound in an open boat by
a southerly gale.

"Expectations vanished," concluded Vancouver when he
reached the head of the sound, which was "encompassed on every
side by the dreary country already described." The party camped in
a windstorm and torrents of rain on a small spot of level ground in a
cove (probably the site of Woodfibre, the mill on the west shore of
the sound). The next day, the boats left this "dreary and comfortless
region," followed along the west shore of Howe Sound and landed
for the night at Gower Point at the western entrance to the sound
(named for Captain Sir Erasmus Gower).

At 4:00 a.m. on June 16, the boats headed northwestward along
the mainland shore, through Welcome Pass and past Thormanby
Island to enter Malaspina Strait. Texada Island was now to the left
of their course. Vancouver thought Texada, because of its length (25
miles), might be a peninsula and he properly deduced that the main
channel through the Strait of Georgia lay on its other side. Beaver
Island (outside Pender Harbour) was the site of this night's camp.
Vancouver described the site as "a tolerably comfortable situation."
Puget's journal gives a different opinion of the camp:

> We brought up for the Night in a Rocky Cove, driven
> there perfectly by Necessity ... it was not till 11 at Night
> that we landed, after a most disagreeable & laborious
> Row, the Boats and their Furniture were all wet nor

was there a Spot to shelter us from the Inclemency
of the Weather, & as it was equally uncomfortable
either remaining in the Water afloat or on Shore most
of us preferred the Ground & Fire for the Remainder
of the Night; from which however we experienced
little or no Inconvenience except the being under the
Necessity of laying down in wet Cloaths.

However uncomfortable the camp, however short the hours of
sleep, the expedition was underway the next morning at 4:00 a.m.
to head up the 50-mile-long Princess Royal and Queens reaches,
past Malibu Rapids to the mountain-enclosed end of Jervis Inlet.
It was to be a day of hopes unrealized. The hope was that this long
inlet might be the sought-after opening to the Northwest Passage.
Vancouver was at first optimistic as the boats entered the steep-
sided inlet:

By the progress we had made this morning ... we
seemed to have penetrated considerably into this
formidable obstacle; and as the more lofty mountains
were now behind us, and no very distant ones were
seen beyond the vallies ... we had great reason to
believe we had passed the centre of this impediment
... and I was induced to hope we should yet find this
inlet winding beyond the mountains.

The inlet was followed until five in the afternoon when, he
wrote with disappointment, "all our hopes vanished, by finding it
terminate, as others had done, in a swampy low land."
Defeat, fatigue and a shortage of food — these were the conditions of the flotilla at the turnaround point of Jervis Inlet beneath

brooding peaks over 7,000 feet high. Puget gives a descriptive account of this day's passage:

> [We] were all day pursuing an Inlet trending to the Northward in a winding Direction & running up between two Inaccessible Ridges & high Snowy Mountains down which immense Water Falls rushed from the very Summits whose Fury largeness and Romantic Appearance is beyond any descriptive Powers I posses[s] ... Some of these Cataracts have nearly a perpendicular descent down Deep Chasms & meeting with frequent Interruptions from projecting Rocks, it greatly adds to the Beauty and View of the Cascades. We pulled as close as possible to one of the largest. The Sea was in a perfect Foam & to look up at its highest discernible Source was absolutely awful & I may add terrific.

I have looked up at those waterfalls, cataracts of tumbling water, gouging and tearing at the steep slopes, uprooting trees and ripping out rocks in their vertical drop to the sea with a noise that sounded like trains rumbling above the cloud-misted cliffs. Saw them as Puget did: "absolutely awful & ... terrific."

The trip up Jervis Inlet to Queens Reach and Princess Louisa Inlet is one of the B.C. coast's most scenic passages. Hundreds of people make this tour each year on private boats or cruise vessels. Both sides of the inlet are bounded by the high summits of the Coast Range with sheer precipices 5,000 to 6,000 feet high. Many of these summits are formed by bare, ice-scraped horns of rock. Snowfields at these higher elevations remain all year.

What was a scenic trip for me in *Kea* must have been a terrible ordeal for the men of the boat expedition. Landing places for rest along the steep shores were infrequent as the shorelines of the inlets are mostly cliffs. But worst of all for them must have been the overwhelming immensity of this mountain-enclosed sea canyon, a place of brooding silence without the comfort of any human presence. This was their background during the long hours they laboured at the oars; stroke, pause, stroke again, as the monotony and physical effort of the hours went on and on and on. A changing view ahead might have given them a renewed spirit — something new to think about, something to anticipate. But everywhere the view was the same: cliff, forest and mountaintop and, looking ahead up the long inlet, they would have been able to see where they would be at the end of the next hour and the hour after that and nothing would change; cliff, forest and mountains as far ahead as they could see.

At the end of Queens Reach, the shortage of food had become critical for the expedition. Hunting had produced the meat of only a few birds — curlews, eagles and crows. Turning, the two boats began to travel back down Queens Reach. Malibu Rapids, the nine-knot entrance to Princess Louisa Inlet, was passed, and it was not until eleven that night that a break in the steep-sided inlet allowed a landing large enough for a camp. Based on their estimated elapsed travel time, this campsite was probably at Patrick Point.

Patrick Point would have been a very uncomfortable and intimidating place to camp, I thought, as I tried to anchor *Kea* off the point. Above it looms the 5,585-foot-high peak of Mount Frederick Williams and offshore, the water is 1,500 feet deep. There is no real beach and the boat crews probably had to sleep in whatever small niches and level spaces they could find beneath the 1,000-foot pinnacle dominating the point. The water off the point was too deep for me to anchor, so to spend the night there I had to tie *Kea* to the shore with two pitons I drove into the rock face of the point.

A strong southerly gale slowed the progress of the boats down Prince of Wales Reach the next day and it was past 9:00 p.m. when camp was made in Goliath Bay at the lower end of the reach. The next day, Puget joined Vancouver in the launch, leaving Thomas Manby in charge of the pinnace. He fell behind and did not notice that Vancouver and Puget headed down Jervis Inlet west of Nelson Island; he turned down Agamemnon Channel along the east shore of the island. Separated from his captain, Manby did the sensible thing: he waited, expecting that Vancouver would come looking for him. Vancouver fired off musket shots in the hope of connecting with Manby but as he was on the other side of Nelson Island, he heard nothing. For three anxious days he remained on the shore of Agamemnon Channel. He wrote:

> In the dark we parted company and did not again meet until we joined the ship in a deplorable state. I remained for three days without a thing to eat but what my Gun afforded, and destitute of a Compass to regain my way to the *Discovery*. My Boat's crew suffered every hardship fatigue and hunger could inflict, in a small cove [where] I passed the night ... that abounded with [mussels]. A fire soon cooked us sufficient to make a voracious Meal of them. In the course of an hour, the whole of us were taken violently ill, and experienced every agony a poisoned set of beings could feel. I gorged them all with hot water which had the desired effect by clearing their stomick from this dangerous food. It threw one man into a fever; the rest fortunately recovered.

Vancouver continued on without Manby and reached the lower end of Jervis Inlet at the prominent cape he named Scotch Fir Point. From there, he crossed Malaspina Strait and ran down the coast of Texada Island, camping for the night of June 20, probably in Anderson Bay as this is the only break along the eastern shore of Texada Island.

Point Upwood (named for a friend of Vancouver) on Texada was passed on June 22 as the boat headed toward Point Grey. When Vancouver reached Point Grey, he was surprised to find the two Spanish ships, the *Sutil* and the *Mexicana,* anchored there, under the command of Valdés and Galiano,

The two Spanish captains had departed from Acapulco, Mexico, in March 1792. Their mission, like Vancouver's, was to find an entrance to the Spanish equivalent of the Northwest Passage, the rumoured Sea of Anian, supposedly discovered by the Greek sailor, Juan de Fuca. On June 6, the two Spanish ships entered the strait bearing his name and, after stopping at Neah Bay, set a course along the inside shore of Vancouver Island. The survey took them through the San Juan Islands, and they named such places as San Juan and Lopez islands and Haro and Rosario straits. They also followed along the continental edge but did not enter Puget Sound. They then went north to an anchorage off Point Grey where the two captains encountered Vancouver on his return from Jervis Inlet. It was not an encounter Vancouver expected or wanted and he wrote: "I cannot avoid acknowledging that, on this occasion, I experienced no small degree of mortification in finding the external shores of the gulf had been visited, and already examined a few miles beyond where my researches during the excursion had extended; making the land, I had been in doubt about, [Texada Island] an island."

Whatever Vancouver's feelings, the ships were there and diplomacy required that he greet the two Spanish captains in a cordial manner. Galiano was able to converse in English and he suggested that Vancouver and his crew remain aboard his ship while a Spanish boat was sent down to Birch Bay for the *Discovery*. Vancouver declined the offer and returned to Birch Bay in the launch. The shoal he passed over south of Point Grey he named Sturgeon Bank because a few sturgeon were purchased there from Natives. Two flood tides and a southerly wind, against which the men rowed for 15 hours, delayed their return and they spent another night camped out off Point Roberts. In the morning of June 23, the launch reached the anchored *Discovery* to conclude this remarkable survey expedition. Puget wrote: "In this Expedition By the Geometrical Mensuration the Boats have run 315 Miles, in 11 Days, on an Average at the Rate of 28 [miles] a Day. This certainly is an Immense Distance, considering the very lumbered and heavy Situation of the Boats on their Outset & the Quality of Articles which must to the End of the Cruise be in them & consequently retard their Progress."

This is a very modest summary of the expedition. Eleven days travelling the open waters of the Strait of Georgia and through the steep-walled canyons of those long, narrow inlets was nothing less than an incredible undertaking. I write this with the authority of having followed the full length of that expedition, an effort for me, even in a comfortable boat, that carried me to the limits of my patience and endurance. My calculations show this round-trip expedition to be nearly 400 miles long, and this in open boats rowed or sailed by men who, at the end of long days, endured nights camped out on stony shores with only a small tent or the clothes they wore for protection. For Vancouver, the expedition further weakened his already fragile health, possibly the onset of a thyroid deficiency.

Manby made it back to the anchored *Discovery* a few days after Vancouver returned. Vancouver gave him such a verbal lashing for negligence that Manby vowed he would never forget "unless he withdraws his words by a satisfactory apology." (Of course, he never did.)

Vancouver was often guilty of sudden and irrational outbursts of temper and violence. The causes were probably fatigue, nervous irritability and poor health. Manby had simply picked a bad time to become separated from Vancouver who, when Manby regained the ship, was exhausted, short-tempered after his long open-boat expedition and particularly vexed with the appearance of the Spaniards. The next day, the *Discovery* and the *Chatham* hauled their anchors in Birch Bay and started north through the Strait of Georgia in company with the two Spanish ships.

I put off following the four ships for a few days to do some exploring on my own. First, I stopped over at the Vancouver Maritime Museum to visit old friends, took a walk along the city's seawall and enjoyed eating at some excellent restaurants. I then left the city, and a stiff wind, blowing out of the southeast, carried *Kea* through the Strait of Georgia toward my destination of Lasqueti Island. I could see it as a distant blue silhouette on the horizon, 35 miles ahead. For six hours I sat at the tiller and steered *Kea* with reefed sails toward that island that never seemed to come closer as the boat rolled, slid and sometimes surfed off the crests of following waves.

Finally, I passed through the narrow, rock-edged slot at the southern tip of the island that opens to the tiny, land-locked harbour of Squitty Bay and tied the boat to the public dock. Then I followed a path that led me to the summit of a point overlooking the bay. Waves rolling in from the open waters of the strait hurled themselves against the point, a tumultuous collision of water against rock. Around me grew a stunted forest of madroña and pine, their branches windblown and bent like the limbs of skinny old men. The point fell away to the sea as a series of rocky terraces that sheltered tiny meadows of wildflowers.

So different, I thought, this solid, rock-formed land from the fluid wild motion of the sea below. Up here, on the dry, windblown and sun-drenched point, the living things were gnarled, spiky and stiff in their reach for the sun. Below me, in the wash and surge of the sea, living things — wet and glistening — lay floating on the sea, their entangled fronds yielding to the power of the waves.

From the point, I watched the advancing front of a rainstorm moving up the strait, black and undershot with the angled shafts of a setting sun. Hurriedly, I returned to the boat just before the storm broke. I stood in the cabin and looked out through rain-streaked windows at my companion in the storm: a great eagle standing on the summit of the point, a silhouette of black under a dark sky, both of us island prisoners of wind and wave.

From Lasqueti, I crossed over to the southern tip of Texada Island and entered Malaspina Strait. Place names I passed along the mainland shore of the strait honour the ships and men engaged in the victory of the British over the French and Spanish fleet at Trafalgar in 1805, an event of interest to me because it was the last major battle of the Royal Navy's sailing ships of war. The place names recalled the heroes of that great battle of wooden ships.

Nelson Island was named for Horatio Nelson, the one-eyed, one-armed admiral who led the British to victory over Napoleon's French and Spanish ships.

Agamemnon Channel carries the name of the first line-of-battle ship Nelson commanded. The *Agamemnon* was also the sixth ship behind Nelson's *Victory* that broke the line of the French-Spanish fleet.

Jervis Inlet to the north of Nelson Island was named for John Jervis who, as the Earl of St. Vincent and First Lord of the Admiralty, saw Nelson as a captain of great promise and gave him the rank of commodore and command at the centres of conflict leading up to the Battle of Trafalgar.

Hardy Island carries the name of Vice-Admiral Sir Thomas Hardy who, as flag captain of Nelson's ship, the *Victory*, was at Nelson's side when he was shot and killed by a French sharpshooter.

And Cape Cockburn, where I anchored for the night, was named for the man who commanded the ship that took Napoleon to his captivity on St. Helena, Admiral Sir George Cockburn.

From Malaspina Strait, I turned around the northern tip of Texada Island and sailed over to tiny Mitlenatch Island where the two tides of Georgia and Queen Charlotte straits meet. *Mitlenatch* is a Comox Native word believed to have meant "calm at the end." This meeting occurs because the Pacific tidal front sweeps into the waters behind Vancouver Island from two directions: from the north, down through Queen Charlotte Strait and Discovery Passage; from the south, in through the Strait of Juan de Fuca and then north through the Strait of Georgia. There is nothing dramatic about the encounter, no swirling waters or wild currents; the two flooding tides — one coming from the south, the other from the north — just meet and turn away from each other to run in the opposite directions of their ebbs.

The tides: They are the eternal clock of the Inland Sea, rising and falling every 6 hours and 20 minutes to flood the shores or leave them bare. They retarded the progress of Vancouver's boat expeditions, which pushed against them with oars, and mine, as I pushed against them with *Kea*'s sails.

The tides come in and the tides go out, twice in each 12-hour, 40-minute tidal cycle, and that simple concept is enough for most people who walk the beach, pilot a boat or go wading. But the tide is more than a story of flooded beaches, dry shores, wet feet or grounded boats. It is the story of a small wave or bulge in the surface of the sea that is lifted by the gravitational attraction of the moon and by the lesser attraction of the sun. As the Earth rotates, the place in the open ocean closest to the moon is lifted by the moon's gravity into the shape of this wave. Relative to the spinning Earth, this wave remains fixed in position beneath the moon, and the Earth slides beneath it. The crest of this wave contains the water of the high tide, low tide follows in the trough behind.

At mid-ocean, the wave is about two feet high. As the wave approaches a shore, its height increases when the shore — like a wedge — slips beneath it. When the wave encounters the restrictions of coastal configurations — estuaries, inlets and straits — its height is greatly increased. Thus, when this wave reaches *Kea*'s home port in lower Puget Sound, it carries with it a high tide of 15 feet.

It is in these currents, rips, overfalls, whirlpools and back eddies of the Inland Sea that the full power of the tides can be seen. In the Gulf Island passages I went through — Active, Porlier and Gabriola passes and Dodd Narrows — I encountered currents as fast as nine knots. My B.C. pilot book warned of the even faster tidal passages I would encounter ahead as I followed Vancouver up the coast: 11 knots in Arran Rapids, Hole-in-the-Wall and Gillard Passage, over

15 knots in Seymour Narrows and 20 knots at Nakwakto Rapids, the fastest sea rapids on the North American continent. With salt water weighing 64 pounds per cubic foot, and millions of cubic feet moving at these speeds through these passages, the power of the tidal currents is incomprehensible.

The theory of the tides is rather academic to the fisherman and the pilot of a boat or a ship. What they want to know is the time of high and low tide, the speed of the tidal currents through constricted channels and the safe times of slack water. This information is contained in the publications of the Canadian Department of Fisheries and Oceans, which covers the waters of the two straits. They are the results of a century-long effort to measure and record the vertical rise and fall of the tides and the time and speed of their horizontal movements.

Does science, with its predictions and measurements, destroy the mystery of the tides, I wondered, as I drifted off Mitlenatch Island. I don't think so. Understanding something of their cause and movements only adds to the sense of awe I feel as I watch their cycles. I knew that were I to return to Mitlenatch Island in 18.6 years, I could watch the same meeting of the tides in height and time. That repetition in the tides is because 18.6 years is the time it takes for the moon to again intersect the Earth's orbit around the sun again and return to the same position.

And it is not only the sea that is affected by the tides, but also my own body, and the atmosphere above. On the flood, the celestial pull of gravity will make my body press infinitesimally less weight on the earth, and overhead, the atmosphere beneath the moon will be lifted to an atmospheric high tide.

A red-streaked dawn greeted me as I left my anchorage at Mitlenatch and sailed up Malaspina Strait toward Cortes Island. The island stood awash in a blood-red sea, an appropriate colour for the blood-stained record of Hernando Cortes, the Spanish conqueror of Mexico, for whom the island was named by Galiano and Valdés as they sailed by in company with Vancouver. The island forms the western shoreline of Desolation Sound, where I anchored amidst the clustered islands of Desolation Sound Marine Park, the Valhalla of the Inland Sea for the summer cruising crowds.

In Desolation Sound, I was torn from the 18th century, where my thoughts had been wandering for over a month, and into the busy, noisy world of a popular yachting destination of this century. All around me were anchored yachts and people scurrying back and forth in rubber boats to cocktail and dinner parties on the decks of palatial yachts. When the noises of the parties subsided, the all-night roar of electrical generators recharging boat batteries began. I fled the clamour of Desolation Sound by anchoring in a far corner and waited there for Vancouver's ships and those of the Spanish captains sailing up from Birch Bay to join me.

XII.

North from Desolation Sound

IT WAS JULY, AND FOR TWO MONTHS VANCOUVER, PUGET,
Broughton, Whidbey and the men of the *Discovery* and the *Chatham*
had relentlessly and thoroughly surveyed the intricacies of the continental edge. Where that shoreline led, they had followed, charting
every twist and turn and every long inlet. Now, as Vancouver left
Birch Bay and headed up the Strait of Georgia, he was accompanied
by the little 46-ton Spanish ships, both only 50 feet long. Vancouver
thought them "the most ill calculated and unfit vessels that could
possibly be imagined for such an expedition."

The question on Vancouver's mind was whether or not a
passage to the ocean lay ahead. Valdés, who spoke a few words of
the Aboriginal language, said that the Natives had told him such a
passage did exist. He was, however, reluctant to believe them.

The northern point of Texada Island in Malaspina Strait was passed and given the name Point Marshall. Harwood and Savary islands were also named. Consistent with Vancouver's bad luck in recognizing rivers, Powell River was seen as only "a small brook." The ships were bounded by the mainland on the right and a string of offshore islands on the left (Hernando, Cortes and lesser islands). Vancouver wrote: "Through this very unpleasant navigation we sailed, still keeping to the continental shore. About dark we entered a spacious sound stretching to the eastward. Here I was very desirous of remaining until day-light; but soundings could not be gained though close to the shore."

The four ships had entered Desolation Sound, a place of no exit for a large sailing ship. The night was dark. It was raining and the winds, wrote Vancouver, were "so light and variable, that by the influence of the tides we were driven about as if we were blindfolded in this labyrinth, until towards midnight, when we were happily conducted to the north side of an island ... where we anchored in company with the *Chatham* and the Spanish vessels, in 32 fathoms water, rocky bottom." The anchorage was on the north side of Kinghorn Island.

In the afternoon, wind drove the four ships off their anchorages at Kinghorn Island and they regrouped at Teakerne Arm on West Redonda Island. There, Vancouver wrote this description of Desolation Sound, which is the source of its name:

> Our situation here was on the northern side of an arm
> of the sound leading to the north-westward, a little
> more than half a mile wide, presenting as gloomy and
> dismal [an] aspect as nature could well be supposed to
> exhibit, had she not been a little aided by vegetation;
> which though dull and uninteresting, screened from

our sight the dreary rocks and precipices that compose
these desolate shores ... Our residence here was truly
forlorn; an awful silence pervaded the gloomy forests,
whilst animated nature seemed to have deserted the
neighboring country.

This site was the anchorage for the four ships for the next 19
days while boat expeditions, both English and Spanish, sought a
way through the daunting complexity of islands and blind inlets
northwest of Desolation Sound.

Imagine an hourglass. The lower part of that glass is the Strait of
Georgia, the upper part Queen Charlotte Strait. The narrow part
of the glass is a huge archipelago of islands numbering in the hundreds. The mainland edge of the archipelago is a fractured coastline
of long, deep inlets that end beneath mountain slopes rising to over
10,000 feet. It is a place of staggering beauty and contrasts. Calm
channels become turbulent rapids and overfalls with a change of
the tide, wind tunnels with a change in the weather. The different shades of light include the gloom of a dark, foreboding fjord,
sun-bright ribbons of water and the filtered grey curtains of fog. I
spent two weeks following the tortuous routes taken by Vancouver,
Johnstone, Broughton, Puget and Whidbey as they threaded this
labyrinth of islands and inlets, by far the most challenging and
scenic part of my voyage. My regret was that the two weeks should
have stretched out to a summer and the summer to a year so that I
could have known this place in all of its seasons and moods.

Historically, these islands and inlets have been the home of a proud and ancient Aboriginal culture. In the mid-years of the 19th century, they were settled by Canadian loggers and fishermen who lived in little floating communities tucked back in the sheltered bays and inlets. For many decades these remote communities provided the fish and timber resources for major British Columbia industries. Today there is still some logging and limited fishing, but on all the islands, there are only a few communities of year-round residents. To call it a sea wilderness is not an exaggeration, and when anchored at night I heard the howl of the wolves, I knew I was amidst islands out of another time.

In many places, my view of islands, forest and sea was identical to the scenes beheld by the original inhabitants of the islands and by the men of the Vancouver expedition. Each island I encountered was a discovery, each with an individuality of its own shoreline, its history and its possibilities.

I travelled alone, an aloneness I enjoyed because it gave me a close intimacy with this seascape, and I lived aboard the boat in a kind of self-imposed simplicity and frugality; just *Kea* and me with all that was needed in food, fuel, shelter and water. By living this way, I felt that I was in closer touch with the men of Vancouver's boat explorations. Like them, I had to carefully ration all my resources; for a drink, just enough from the water jug for half a glass with none wasted; for a bath, only a pot of water; and leftovers from dinner eaten for the next day's lunch. The smallest things became very special: the can of fish in the rice that made of it a feast; the half-portion of the chocolate bar, a treat; the one rum drink before dinner and the one pipe afterwards, a luxury. That life of enforced simplicity and frugality among the islands cleared my mind and I became more receptive to every nuance of the voyage: a change in the weather, the reversal of a tidal current, the heat of the sun, the damp coldness of fog. Each point I rounded opened new and surprising views and discoveries that were of both past and present. Those discoveries were made with my eyes, ears and nose tuned to the messages expressed around me in wind, rock and tide, and by the immutable laws of nature where the drama of all living things is the harsh miracle of survival.

As I wandered through the islands in silence and isolation, I began to talk to whomever or whatever might be listening. And so I held conversations with eagles, mink, deer, river otter, bears, sea birds and the dead snags I thought of as ancient totem poles. Such were my experiences in this magnificent seascape, an altogether different experience from that of Vancouver's men who had to force their way through this labyrinth of passages to find an open route to the sea.

Through the Labyrinth

THE SEARCH FOR A PASSAGE TO THE SEA BEGAN WITH JOHNSTONE rowing and sailing up Toba Inlet, Ramsay Arm and Bute Inlet (named for John Stuart, Earl of Bute) on a round-trip expedition of seven days and over 200 miles. All three of the inlets are dead ends.

Two days later, in two boats provisioned for one week, Johnstone, master's mate Selma Swine and Menzies set out again to follow a tortuous route that led them to the open waters of Queen Charlotte Strait. From Teakerne Arm, they went up Lewis and Calm channels and through the Yuculta, Dillard, Dent and Greene Point rapids to reach Cordero Channel. Frederick and Phillips arms and then Loughborough Inlet (after Baron Loughborough) were explored to their ends. In Loughborough Inlet the men camped on a small island but were roused from their sleep by the rising tide. Menzies described that uncomfortable night:

In the middle of the night they were hastily roused
from their repose by the flowing of the Tide, which
had risen so much higher than they expected and
rushed upon them so suddenly, that every person got
completely drenched before they could remove to
the higher ground. This little disaster rendered them
so uncomfortable for the remainder of the night that
they could not enjoy their slumber but anxiously look
forward to day break to depart.

The strong flood tides were coming from the north and this
convinced Johnstone that the channel he was following led to the
ocean somewhere ahead. The next day, the boats went up Wellbore
Channel and through Whirlpool Rapids. Turning down Sunderland
Channel, Johnstone and his crew then entered the strait now
bearing his name that leads to Queen Charlotte Strait and the open
Pacific. Vancouver, summarizing Johnstone's report of his voyage,
wrote the conclusion to this difficult but significant voyage:

In the hope of reaching the westernmost island in sight,
and by that means of determining the great object of their
pursuit, they proceeded with a fresh gale from the east,
attended by a great fall of rain, until midnight; when,
supposing themselves at the limits they had seen before
it was dark, they came to a grapnel under the lee of a
small island, which in some degree sheltered them from
the inclemency of the night. This extremely unpleasant
weather continued without intermission, the whole days
out of the seven for which they had been provided, and
the small remains of their stock were becoming hourly
more insufficient for the distant voyage they had yet

to perform in returning to the ships ... but a westerly
wind and pleasant weather returning ... they rowed to
an island [probably Pine Island] conspicuously situated,
from whence their expectations were gratified by a clear
though distant view of the expansive ocean.

The passage to the sea had been found, but at this point, the
boats were 120 miles away from the *Discovery* anchored in Teakerne
Arm. The return journey was made in the remarkably short time of
only two days. Menzies described the condition of Johnstone and
his crews upon their return: "They had hastened night & day to join
the Ships ... harassed with hunger & fatigue being for the last two
days upon a single scant meal & without any rest or out of the Boats
for the last 24 hours."

Johnstone's boat expedition was one of the most difficult explorations of the survey and the one that determined that Vancouver
Island was an island.

I left the busy summer yachting scene of Desolation Sound and followed Johnstone's track up Lewis and Calm channels, apprehensive
about the series of five rapids that lay ahead. I had studied the complicated tables that predicted the time of slack water at each of the
rapids. Read them once, twice and three times because these tables
are more than exercises in simple arithmetic. In a tide-running
rapid, they are equations for survival.

At Yuculta Rapids, I waited out the last of the flood, then charged
up against the weakening current as fast as the little 10-horsepower

diesel engine could push the boat. Was I late? Was I early? No matter; I was committed and could only hope that I would reach the top of Yuculta in time to pass through the other two rapids of Gillard and Dent on the same slack current. To my surprise, I was right on time; water calm, current nil, and I passed safely through the first three rapids.

Greene Point, the next rapid, was some 10 miles ahead with a slack-water time earlier than the Gillard and Dent rapids because its ebb turns earlier. After my first success, I was bold, and determined to get through it without an overnight stop between the two rapids. But I was late and so I got the full effect of the Greene Point Rapids. The currents, overfalls and the outer edges of whirlpools grabbed *Kea* with invisible claws and sent it spinning and bobbing down the channel. Long, sliding back eddies caught it in strong countercurrents to shoot it back up the channel, completely out of my control.

Shaken by that experience, I anchored in the first cove I could find. That night, I slept uneasily as I contemplated the next rapid I had to pass through, the one with the ominous name of Whirlpool Rapids in Wellbore Channel. I had nightmares about a black hole in the water rotating around a vortex of swirling water that would suck the helpless boat into its funnel-like centre stern first, before spitting it out. Edgar Allen Poe described such a whirlpool in his chilling narrative *A Descent into the Maelstrom*. It reads: "The boat appeared to be hanging, as if by magic, midway down, upon the interior surface of a funnel vast in circumference, prodigious in depth and whose perfectly smooth sides might have been mistaken for ebony, but for the bewildering rapidity with which they spun around in a flood of golden glory along the black walls, and far away down into the most inmost recesses of the abyss."

But Whirlpool Rapid was not even visible the next day and, with relief, I entered windy Sunderland Channel, which led me to an anchorage at Tuna Point in Johnstone Strait. I had found my way there by following Johnstone, but I would have liked to follow him back to Desolation Sound so that I could run the entire passage again.

XIV.

Discovery Passage

WHILE JOHNSTONE HAD BEEN EXPLORING TO THE NORTH, PUGET and Whidbey had crossed over to the Vancouver Island shore of the Strait of Georgia and, rounding Cape Mudge, they entered Discovery Passage. Vancouver surmised correctly that this passage connected with the one found by Johnstone and would lead to the sea.

On the morning of July 14, the *Discovery* and the *Chatham* cleared Desolation Sound, leaving behind the Spanish ships. The two ships rounded Cape Mudge (honouring Zachary Mudge) and anchored in Menzies Bay just below Seymour Narrows. It was a pleasant sail after the gloom of Desolation Sound and Vancouver wrote: "The wind continued light from the northern quarter, and the weather being serene and pleasant, made a most agreeable change. Numberless whales enjoying the season, were playing about the ship in every direction ... Indians visited us in several canoes, with young birds, mostly sea fowl, fish, and some berries, to barter for our trinkets and other commodities."

A strong flood tide coming down Seymour Narrows was further evidence of an open channel to the northwest. Puget and Whidbey went ahead in the launch and the cutter to determine if there were any obstructions that might be hazardous to the ships. When it was found to be open to navigation, the two ships sailed through Seymour Narrows.

Two-mile-long Seymour Narrows, less than a half-mile wide, is the most dangerous passage on the British Columbia coast. Tidal currents run up to 16 knots and the eddies, whirlpools and back-currents are extremely threatening, but through this turbulent water, Vancouver was able to sail the slow, awkward, wind-driven, 99-foot, 337-ton *Discovery*. Sailing with an opposing northwest wind but with a strong ebb tide, he was able to drift and tack through the narrows in a remarkable display of seamanship. Of this passage, Vancouver wrote only that "with pleasant weather and a fresh breeze at NW we weighed about three o'clock, turned through the narrows, and, having gained about three leagues by the time it was nearly dark, we anchored on the western shore in a small bay."

In the years since that passage, at least 25 large ships and over 100 fishboats, tugs and yachts have been wrecked or sunk in Seymour Narrows with a recorded loss of 114 lives. The tremendous rush of water flowing through the constriction of the half-mile-wide passage creates immense turbulence, cross-currents and whirlpools 30 to 40 feet in diameter. For only a few minutes during the slack-water period between the changes of the tides can most ships and boats safely pass through the narrows.

Until 1958, the notorious Ripple Rock stood in mid-channel, adding to the danger of the passage. The rock was removed by blasting in 1958 and the explosion, at the time, was the largest non-nuclear blast ever detonated. On April 15, 2,756,324 pounds of explosives were detonated in the hollowed-out dome of the rock. The blast was followed by a 1,000-foot exploding tower of water, mud and rock. After the explosion, the twin summits of Ripple Rock were 47 and 69 feet beneath the surface of the water.

After transiting the narrows, the *Discovery* and the *Chatham* anchored in Elk Bay across from the opening to Okisollo Channel. The next ebb carried the ships around Chatham Point (after John Pitt, second Earl of Chatham) and into Johnstone Strait. The strait, 90 miles long and only a few miles wide, is like a wind tunnel with waves particularly high when northwest winds blow down the strait against an ebbing tide. This was the condition Vancouver encountered, writing: "The length of coast ... forms a channel which, though narrow, is fair and navigable; manifested by the adverse winds obliging us to beat to windward every foot of the channel, and to perform a complete traverse [tack] from shore to shore through its whole extent."

Tack and turn, then tack again, over and over, as the two ships crawled their way through the strait. A few temporary anchorages were found in small coves where the ships could stop to await favourable tides but, wrote Vancouver, "We were very apprehensive of losing, by the adverse tide, all we had gained by the favorable stream; I not having been able to reach the bottom [to anchor] with 100 fathoms [600 feet] of line."

Slowly, the two ships advanced through Johnstone Strait. In the small bay formed by the mouth of the Adams River, both ships grounded under their sterns. Both got off without difficulty and continued sailing through the strait. (Two islands in the strait were named: Thurlow Island for Baron Thurlow and Hardwick Island for the Earl of Hardwick.)

Puget and Whidbey were sent to explore Port Neville and Broughton in the *Chatham* was ordered to explore Havannah Channel. Vancouver continued to sail up the strait to an Aboriginal village at the mouth of the Nimpkish River. He spent three days there, his men trading sheet copper and woollen cloth for over 200 otter skins. Vancouver would not offer the natives what they most wanted, guns and ammunition, which, he felt, "humanity, prudence and policy directed to be withheld." He then crossed over to an appointed rendezvous off Hanson Island in the northern end of Johnstone Strait to await the return of Puget and Broughton.

The Broughton Archipelago

VANCOUVER AND HIS TWO SHIPS HAD FOUGHT THE WIND AND tides of Johnstone Strait, and so did *Kea* and I in the short run we made from Tuna Point to Port Neville. The wind was out of the south, blowing up the strait, and the tide was on a fast ebb. We had never sailed so fast: 12 knots on a wild run that took us to Port Neville. Half of that speed was because of the gale pushing us, the other half because of the tide carrying us.

Puget and Whidbey had made a brief exploration of Port Neville, but it proved to be an unimportant inlet not worthy of any special comment. What was unimportant for them is my favourite port of the Inland Sea.

I tied up at Port Neville's wind-protected government dock. A few fishboats were moored next to me, their owners ready for the brief, 24-hour fishing period that would open the next morning. I asked one of the fishermen what he thought his chances of catching a fish would be during this short opening. He laughed, telling me that he had paid three dollars a gallon for fuel and — if he caught any fish at all — he would get only two dollars per pound of fish.

"Fishing has nothing to do with earning a living any more," he said, "but it's the only thing I know or care about. It's what I have been doing for 40 years and I can't change." The name of his boat fit his life and his philosophy: *Obsession.*

That fisherman — and many like him — was possessed and captivated by the sea from which he tried to make his living. There, in the rhythms of tides, weather and the migrations of fish and birds, is an order he understands. His life, his profession, is a response of the human heart to these things and to something more profound and larger than the single life of the individual trying to earn a living.

Something of that feeling must have been handed down through the four generations of the Hansen family that have lived in Port Neville. The family founded the old store, which at one time served the settlers, loggers and fishermen of the surrounding area. Only Lorna, granddaughter of the founding Hansens, and her daughter still live at Port Neville. The original log store, its weathered sign reading "1924," is closed, its interior a quiet refuge for old papers and empty bins and shelves no longer stacked with the groceries and supplies of an outpost community. Lorna is doing what she can with her limited means to keep the store standing as a memorial to the family. The old barn still stands, and a few chickens peck around the edges of a deer-fenced garden. Slowly the forest is creeping inward around the fields no longer mowed, and bear and cougar wander just behind the foliage of green. As I walked around Port Neville, I saw it as a place of harmony and continuity, a place that has marked time through more than a century of family generations.

The next morning, I started *Kea*'s engine and the light indicating low oil pressure turned red. I checked the oil-measuring stick and it showed the oil level at the full mark. One of the fishermen at the Port Neville dock took a look at the engine, shook his head, and said, "Guess you better go see Doug in Port Harvey, just up the coast. He can fix anything."

I sailed *Kea* along the nine-mile shoreline of Johnstone Strait into Port Harvey and to what I thought had to be Doug's place: a long, floating log wharf supporting a collection of rusted engines, spools of cable and stacks of lumber. Doug, dressed in bib overalls and a plaid shirt, came down to greet me. I introduced myself and explained my problem. Without hesitating, no excuses like "too busy now," he jumped aboard the boat, lifted off the engine cover and studied the engine.

"Have you lost oil pressure before?" he asked.

"No, it just happened this morning when I tried to start the engine."

"Maybe the problem is the oil pump," he said. "I'll take it out and look at it."

To take the pump out, Doug had to make a special tool to loosen an odd-diameter nut. He spent an hour or so in his shop making the tool, then all afternoon taking the oil pump apart and putting it back together again. Still no oil pressure when he started the engine, and I began to think about the mounting hourly costs. For the rest of that day, Doug fiddled with the engine but was unable to find the cause of the oil pressure problem.

The next morning when he came down to the boat, he just sat and studied the engine. The only thing he hadn't checked was the little oil filter. He unscrewed it from the engine, reamed it out with a screwdriver, replaced it with a new one and started the engine; no red light, oil pressure normal.

Doug had spent something like 12 hours working on the engine and I expected his bill would be fairly high.

"So what do I owe you, Doug?"

"You owe me $7.50; that's the price of that filter."

"Come on, Doug, what do I owe you?"

"That's all," he said. "I should have checked that filter first thing and because I didn't, you don't have to pay me for my ignorance."

Doug had hung his jacket on a post. When he bent over to wash his hands, I slipped $150 in the pocket of his jacket and got underway before he found it.

Broughton examined Port Harvey, which opens to Havannah Channel. Keeping the mainland to the right — the command for all the exploratory voyages — he traced out the shoreline of Call Inlet (named after Sir John Call) and then anchored outside Chatham Channel. The opening to this narrow, tide-running channel is barely a few yards wide, and Broughton must have worried about endangering his ship if he tried to enter. The flood tide running through it, however, was proof that it led to some large, unseen interior arm of the sea and Broughton was duty-bound to follow wherever it led. The next morning, the *Chatham*'s boats towed the ship safely through the passage to begin Broughton's 10-day exploration of the huge maze of islands Vancouver named in his honour, the Broughton Archipelago.

An ancient tree stands at the entrance to Chatham Channel, its limbs wind-shattered and bent. That tree, I thought, was a living witness to the passage of a small wooden ship over two centuries ago towed through the channel by men labouring at the oars of their boats. For the *Chatham* and the men at the oars, that would not have been an easy passage. Nor was it for me as I bucked an opposing tide through the pass. To stay in mid-channel, and to avoid the thick kelp beds that lined both sides of the passage, I had to keep the boat's course lined up between two shore beacons that marked the course. Then, the channel widened and I relaxed and counted the many bears that came down to the shoreline to roll and turn rocks as they grubbed for food.

Broughton exited Chatham Channel and turned up Knight Inlet (honouring British Admiral Sir John Knight). From Broughton's report, Vancouver wrote a description of what he encountered in Knight Inlet: "The shore of it, like most of those lately surveyed, is formed by high stupendous mountains rising almost perpendicularly from the water's edge. The dissolving snow on their summits produced many cataracts that fell with great impetuosity down their barren rugged sides. The fresh water that thus descended gave a pale white hue to the channel, rendering its content entirely fresh at the head, and drinkable for twenty miles below it."

I travelled only partway up Knight Inlet, just far enough to get some feeling for what Broughton and his men might have experienced in sailing up the huge fjord. I imagine that they — like me — were intimidated by this two-mile-wide canyon of space bordered by twin shorelines rising to elevations of 5,000 feet. It is these steep shores, climbing abruptly from the water's edge, that frame the inlet and give depth and distance to its vast panorama of water, sky and mountain. What worried me — and probably Broughton — was that this mountain-enclosed inlet could become a wind-canyon of compressed intensity that could trap a vessel. If such a wind were to develop, that vessel would have few places of shelter along the steep shores and no place to anchor, because the depths of the inlet in many places exceed 1,800 feet. So, after only a half-day of sailing, I turned and made a hasty retreat back down Knight Inlet to Minstrel Island.

The island and nearby Sambo Point and Bones Bay were named because of the minstrel shows staged by crew members of the ship HMS *Amethyst*, which visited the island in 1876. "Mr. Bones" and "Sambo" were two characters in the black-faced minstrel cast performing for a probably amazed group of loggers and Kwakiutl First Nations.

Logging was the major industry around the island in the early part of the last century and Minstrel Island became a busy community with a hotel, stores, a boatyard, a machine ship and a scheduled Union Steamship stop. The arrival of the steamship and Saturday-night dances were events to celebrate and the hotel saloon had the unofficial record of serving more beer than any other pub in British Columbia. Today, sadly, little of the old community survives, and both the old hotel and store are gone.

After surveying Knight Inlet, Broughton entered Tribune Channel to follow along the mainland shore. Vancouver relates his difficult voyage westward through Tribune Channel: "A passage through this channel was accomplished on the 25th, notwithstanding the wind was very fickle, and blew hard in squalls, attended with much lightening, thunder and rain; the night was nearly calm, gloomy and dark; and not being able to gain soundings, although within thirty yards of the rocky shores, they were driven about as the current of the tides directed, and happily escaped, though surrounded on all sides by innumerable rocks and rocky islets."

On July 27, Broughton reached the western opening of Tribune Channel and passed a prominent point he named Deep Sea Bluff. The *Chatham* then sailed through Raleigh Passage, headed west through Fife Sound (after James Duff, second Earl of Fife) to Queen Charlotte Strait and to the *Discovery* anchored off Hanson Island.

I followed Broughton through Tribune Channel by way of narrow Sergeant Passage, which separates Viscount Island from the mainland. Suddenly, from a warm, sun-lit day, I was travelling through a cool, shadowed canyon with the steep side of the island looming 2,000 feet above me.

Rounding Irvine Point, I entered Wahkana Bay, where I anchored for the night. The little bay, with its dark, forested shoreline, was so quiet that I tiptoed around the decks barefooted so as not to break the windless silence. The only thing moving was the tide, slowly dropping and soundless. If I listened very closely, I thought, I would probably have been able to hear the trees growing.

In the evening, the silence was shattered by the flash of tiny fish leaping out of the sea like tiny pebbles skittering across the water as they frantically tried to escape a river otter. The otter dove after them and the fish leaped clear of the water, some even landing on the shore. In the middle of the night, I got up to pee over the side. I first thought that the black water beneath me was reflecting hundreds of overhead stars and then I realized the splashing was activating hundreds of phosphorescent organisms to make a galaxy of light in the black water.

A classic coastal morning dawned the next day as I headed down Tribune Channel. Mist hung in the air and draped the hills and the sea with a soft covering of grey-green luminosity. It was that scene of a mystical fog-washed fjord that artists try to capture in paint, but I was looking at the original and natural masterpiece.

But there were flaws in the scene: the clear-cuts that in places savaged the hills, leaving behind tangles of broken limbs and water-eroded gullies. I watched as an orange helicopter — looking like a huge bug — plucked bundles of logs off a steep hillside with a long cable. It then dropped to sea level and released the bundles, which hit the water in a huge splash. The helicopter than returned for another load and I timed its round trip at less than five minutes. Five minutes to pluck from the hillside the many years of growing trees whose lives concluded with their brief aerial journey.

A few miles farther on, I reached the steep, conspicuous point Broughton named Deep Sea Bluff. It stands as a sharp, high promontory that rises straight up out of the sea. I paused for a few moments beneath the bluff, thinking to myself that they came to this place, those men with Broughton, looked up at the same rock face I was seeing and passed on, a moment enshrined forever in the name they left behind for the bluff.

XVI.

Deep Sea Bluff

BROUGHTON HAD SURVEYED THE CONTINENTAL EDGE WESTWARD
to Deep Sea Bluff and then rejoined Vancouver at the rendezvous
of Hanson Island. His voyage, however, had bypassed a long section
of the mainland shore. To fill in this gap, Vancouver left the Hanson
Island anchorage on July 28 and, with the *Chatham*, entered the
western entrance to Fife Sound. The two points at the entry to the
sound were named Duff and Gordon (after Alexander Gordon,
fourth Duke of Gordon and a close friend of James Duff).

Two miles into the sound, the two ships anchored along the
southern shore of Broughton Island, probably just off Wicklow
Point. On the morning of the 29th Vancouver wrote:

> We were under sail, with a light favorable breeze, suffi-
> cient to have carried us at the rate of near a league per

hour; yet the ship remained stationary and ungovern-
able, not answering to her helm in any direction.
In this very unpleasant and disagreeable situation,
attributed by us to a kind of under tow, or counter tide,
we continued until near dark when, a most powerful
breeze springing up, we reached Deep Sea Bluff, and
anchored about eleven at night in a small opening on
its western side in 70 fathoms of water.

Deep Sea Bluff stands at the opening to Simoom Sound. The following day, the two ships moved into the sound for wood and water.
Menzies reported that in two casts of the seine net, nearly a hundred
salmon were caught. Vancouver in the yawl went to O'Brien Bay
at the end of the sound. A narrow isthmus lies between O'Brien
Bay and the lower part of Kingcome Inlet. Vancouver walked the
few steps across the isthmus to a view of both Kingcome Inlet and
Sutlej Channel. It was, I imagine, a most disturbing view because
out there, beyond O'Brien Bay, he could see that ahead lay more
difficult and tedious days and miles charting the mainland.

For me, Simoom Sound, like Deep Sea Bluff, was a special place
because it gave me another fixed geographic "touching point" with
the expedition. It was from the small stream in the sound across
from Esther Point that men filled their water casks. I landed on the
narrow beach there and, symbolically, filled two jugs of water from
the same stream into which they had dipped their buckets.

I then went to O'Brien Bay, where Vancouver walked across the narrow Wishart Peninsula to look out over the waters beyond. There were no alternative routes for me to take when I followed his walk across the narrow isthmus, just the one taken by Vancouver himself. For the historian, footstep by footstep, it is a short walk to be savoured.

On July 31, a boat expedition began that would follow along the shoreline of the most complicated section of the mainland shore yet encountered. That it was followed — every mile of it — through reef and rock, through tide-rushing narrows in dismal, rainy weather is testament to the dedication of Vancouver and his men to chart this twisting, turning coast.

The four officers participating were Vancouver, Broughton and Puget in the launch and Whidbey in the cutter. While these officers and their boat crews were gone, the men aboard the *Discovery* and the *Chatham* were kept busy brewing spruce beer and filling their water casks at the small creek in Simoom Sound.

The weather was awful, "dark and gloomy ... with frequent loud Claps of Thunder preceded by vivid flashes of lightening," wrote Menzies. A hunting party shot cormorants nesting on the cliffs of Deep Sea Bluff.

The boat parties were enduring the same bad weather as they followed along the shoreline of mile-wide Kingcome Inlet, which ends beneath the lofty, 6,000-foot summits of the Kingcome Mountains. The boats would have been insignificant in the deep, sea-filled chasm of the inlet beneath lowering skies of gloom and rain. A cold, wet camp for the night was made on the narrow and rocky beach at the mouth of Charles Creek. The next day, equally forbidding Wakeman Sound was surveyed.

The exploration of these two large inlets was but a prelude to what was to come as the two boats were rowed or sailed through Sutlej Channel and into Grappler Sound. The boats then entered a narrow passage in the upper end of the sound, which took them to the broken, rock-infested, far northern corner of the Broughton Archipelago. I was afraid to take *Kea* beyond that passage to follow the boats because, sailing alone, I had no one standing on the bow to watch for rocks. Vancouver had to go through that passage because the mainland shore went that way. Narrow and shallow Hopetown Pass led him into Mackenzie Sound, where "the stupendous mountains on each side of this narrow chasm, prevented a due circulation of air below, by excluding the rays of the sun; whilst exhalations from the surface of the water and the humid shores wanting rarefaction, were, in a great measure, detained, like steam in a condensed state; the evaporation thus produced a degree of cold and chillness which rendered our night's lodging very unpleasant."

One of those mountains, Mount Stephens, "conspicuous for its irregular form, and its elevation above the rest of the hills" is 5,665 feet high. Vancouver called Mackenzie Sound "a chasm in the mountains, caused by some violent efforts of nature." Apparently, he was unaware of the effects of glacial carving, which formed the many sounds and inlets along the continental shore.

Mackenzie Sound was exited through Kenneth Passage and described as "excessively dangerous, owing to the number of rocky islets, sunken rocks, and, the tides setting through it with great rapidity and irregularity."

There was another dangerous passage ahead as the boats came down Wells Passage (honouring Admiral Sir John Wells) and entered Stuart Narrows, the opening to 12-mile-long Drury Inlet. Puget described their passage through Stuart Narrows:

> About Two Miles and a half Westward of the Channel that leads into the Sound we were alarmed with a most Violent Roar, where the Inlet was contracted by two projecting Islands to ½ Mile and before the Boat could pull either one way or the other we were hurried through a most Rapid fall nor had we even time to Sound. It was apparently occasioned by Sunken Rocks and the Vortex was so great that the Launch was taken round and Round notwithstanding every Effort to the Contrary.

At the head of Drury Inlet, a Native village was found and Puget's description of it provides a good picture of what such a community looked like, in what was probably a first Aboriginal–European contact:

> In the Afternoon ... we found a large Indian Village situated on an Elevated Bank ... This Village consisted of three separate Rows of Buildings at Top [of the bank] between which was a Narrow Lane or Path to admit an Intercourse from house to house ... The Outside and Roof were composed of large Pine Plank & indeed they seem well calculated to Defend their Inhabitants from the Inclemency of either Wind or Weather. In each of the Houses is a large Fire, for the Convenience of Cooking, which is performed by hot Stones among Water to Boil either Whale, Porpoise or Seal, on which three they principally live ... Strong Rancid Oil

extracted from those Marine Animals is used as Sauce with this Food ... Both Sexes appear to live indiscriminately with each in the Same room. I do not mean that the Women have no Separate Apartments, indeed to do them justice I have heard splendid Offers being made [by his crew] to tempt their Chastity but it never succeeded & they are equally adverse to hear language or see Signs made to express our Meaning on those Occasions, some I have seen cry.

At the village, Vancouver left Puget and Whidbey to explore the rest of Drury Inlet and returned with Broughton to the *Discovery* and the *Chatham*, both anchored off Simoom Sound. Boyles Point (named for Captain Charles Boyles of the Royal Navy), at the west entrance to Wells Passage, had been established as the rendezvous point for the return of Puget and Whidbey. These two continued the exploration of Drury Inlet to its terminus in the reversing falls of Tsibass Lagoon at the end of Actaeon Sound. From Puget's and Whidbey's report, Vancouver wrote this description of the tide-running, rock-scattered inlet:

Near its termination, they pursued a very narrow opening on its northern shore, winding towards the E.N.E. replete with overfills and sunken rocks, and ending by a cascade ... These are perfectly salt, and seem to own their origin to the tidal waters, which in general, rise seventeen feet, and, at high water, render these falls imperceptible, as the bar or obstruction, at that time, lies from four to six feet beneath the surface of sea, and consequently at low water causes a fall of ten or twelve feet; some of which are twenty yards in width.

In the afternoon of the following day, the two ships sailed south out of Simoom Sound, through Raleigh Passage and down Fife Sound heading toward the rendezvous site where Puget and Whidbey were met. With the wind falling calm, the two ships anchored off the Polkinghorne Islands just outside the entry to Wells Passage. The expedition had reached Queen Charlotte Strait and, with what must have been great relief, Vancouver was able to write: "By this expedition, the continental shore was traced to the westernmost land in sight. We had now only to proceed along it, as soon as the wind and weather would permit our moving."

With islands to the left, to the right, ahead and behind me, I left the anchored ships in Simoom Sound. They were part of a cluster of hundreds of islands and islets at the outer edge of the Broughton Archipelago where it meets Queen Charlotte Strait. The chart of the area showed a fly-specked pattern of islands and narrow, winding channels separating one from another.

With no lookout forward to sight my way through the rocks and reefs of these passages, I travelled the maze at something less than a walker's pace, checking off on the chart each island I rounded, with such evocative names as Seabreeze, Jumble, Puzzle and Mist. Two other island names suggested to me the spirit and essence of this stunning marine landscape: Midsummer and Eden. The rather prosaic name of Joe Cove was where I anchored on Eden Island, Spring Passage where I anchored on Midsummer Island.

On my last night in this island group, I anchored off Mound Island. There is a small beach at one corner of the island where I went ashore and slept for the night on a green, mossy mound that covered an ancient kitchen midden, built up over thousands of years from the discarded shells of Aboriginal island dwellers. On that night on that beach, watching the surrounding islands fade in the gathering darkness to then be relit by a rising moon, I felt that I had come to the heart, soul and spirit of my voyage. On that island of a Native culture, which I had reached on a voyage of maritime history, I felt that I was a presence that in some way joined the two histories, and that I had been able to make a connection to both in that Eden of islands I travelled through in midsummer.

I would have stayed longer among those islands but Queen Charlotte Strait had yet to be explored, following Vancouver's track to Cape Caution, some 60 miles to the northwest. His ships had encountered the hazardous rocks and reefs of the strait and I went looking for two of those rocks: the ones that had nearly wrecked the *Discovery* and the *Chatham*.

XVII.

To Cape Caution

IN THE AFTERNOON OF AUGUST 6, THE TWO SHIPS SAILED INTO Queen Charlotte Strait under a light breeze that advanced them a few miles west from Boyles Point. Their course, about three miles off the mainland, placed them sailing through Richards Channel. The next morning the wind died, and fog covered the water, "a very thick fog," wrote Vancouver, "that obscured every surrounding object until noon, without our being able to gain soundings; so that we were left to the mercy of the currents, in a situation that could not fail to occasion the most anxious solicitude." A light breeze blew the fog away and then the *Discovery* grounded on a hidden reef on an ebbing tide.

Immediately, signals were made to the *Chatham* and boats were sent over to assist. The attempt to pull the ship off the rock by hauling on an anchor failed. With the tide rapidly dropping, topmasts and yards were taken down and used to shore up the ship.

Water, wood and stone ballast were dumped overboard. The ship had grounded under its bow but the stern section floated. In this dangerous position, it swung around by the stern and leaned at an alarming angle. Fortunately, there was very little swell or the ship would have been wrecked as it lay immobile on the reef, its bow high and dry. Wrote Vancouver: "In this melancholy situation, we remained, expecting relief from the returning flood, which to our inexpressible joy was at length announced by the floating of the shoars [shears], a happy indication of the ship righting ... about two in the morning ... when the ship becoming nearly upright, we hove on the stern cable, and, without any particular efforts, or much strain, had the inexpressible satisfaction of feeling her again float, without having received the least apparent injury."

Manby gave a more vivid account of the grounding:

> While standing through a dangerous sound, the ship struck on a reef which soon left her immovable. The yards and top masts were struck and got over in hopes of preventing her tumbling over. After laying upright half an hour, the breeze died away, and calm following cheered our spirits up with the enlivening hope the flowing tide might again float her if the rocks had not pierced her bottom. Seven long and tedious hours we saw on the ship's side without the ability of giving her any assistance but that of carrying out an anchor and three cables, ready to heave upon at high water. At ten at night she considerably righted, and soon after so much that we could stand the deck and bring cables to the capstan, which had the desired effect, and hove us into deep water at 12 o'clock without any other loss than that part of the false keel and gripe.

By noon the next day, order was restored aboard the ship and cautiously it got under way through a channel Vancouver described as "not more than half a mile wide, bounded on one side by islands [the Southgate Group], rocks and breakers which in some places appeared almost to meet the continental edge."

By 6:00 p.m., the *Discovery* had cleared the most difficult part of the channel and then the *Chatham* grounded. Boats from the *Discovery* were immediately sent to assist. Wrote Vancouver: "Thus, before we had recovered from the fatiguing exertions and anxious solicitude of one distressing night, the endurance of a similar calamity was our portion for the next. I had less reason at first to hope for the preservation of the *Chatham* under the circumstances of her disaster ... as the oceanic swell was here very perceptible."

When the *Chatham* was later hauled in Nootka Sound, the damage was seen to be limited to the forefoot and false keel and a few torn sheets of copper.

Richards Channel, the area of the groundings, is less than a mile wide between the Jeanette Islands and offshore Ghost Island. Menzies wrote that the *Discovery* grounded on a rock at 50° 5' north latitude. This line exactly crosses a cluster of small rocks awash just off Ghost Island and it was one of these the *Discovery* hit.

As I circled that group of deadly rocks, I thought what a disaster it would have been for the expedition if the *Discovery* had been lost. The *Chatham*, of course, after working free of the rock it grounded on, could have come to the rescue of *Discovery*'s men. But then what? The *Chatham* was a much smaller ship and adding the 162 men rescued from the *Discovery* to the *Chatham*'s 76 would have overcrowded the ship and put a severe strain on its food and water. The nearest port of possible rescue would have been Nootka Sound on the west coast of Vancouver Island where arrangements could probably have been made with a visiting ship to return the men to England.

But the loss of the ship would have been devastating. All the results of the survey, Vancouver's journal and his carefully drawn charts might have gone down with the ship, along with the specimens of plants Menzies had been collecting. Ship wrecked, mission unaccomplished; for Vancouver, that would have meant the mandatory court martial for the loss of a ship, and a reputation ruined.

Fog enclosed the ships the next day as they were steering toward Europa Passage and the more open waters of Queen Charlotte Strait. Out there and in fog, Vancouver missed the two openings of Schooner and Slingsby channels leading to Seymour and Belize inlets. If they had been seen, they would have had to be explored by ships' boats and that exploration would have taken the boats through the dangerous Nakwakto Rapids, and then along the 75-mile shoreline of the two inlets.

Europa Passage provided a safe way between the Storm Islands and Pine Island and the two ships came to anchor off the entrance to Shadwell Passage between Hope and Nigei islands. This was the last Inland Sea anchorage for the two ships. The next day, August 10, they exited Queen Charlotte Strait and sailed around Cape Caution to conclude the 104-day exploration of the Strait of Juan de Fuca, Puget Sound, the Strait of Georgia and Queen Charlotte Strait.

The last night of my voyage was spent at the head of Schooner Channel, where I had gone to look at Nakwakto Rapids. On the ebb tide, all the accumulated waters of Seymour and Belize inlets rush through the narrow passage of the rapids. The passage is further constricted by the small island standing in the centre of the rapids, nicknamed "Tremble Island" because it is reported to tremble as this massive tidal current flows around it. Graffiti painted on the island boasts such messages as "I spent the night on Tremble Island." On my voyage, I had safely transited five rapids, but I did not want to get even close to the thundering water pouring through Nakwakto Rapids.

Rain was falling back in narrow Schooner Channel where I anchored. A low mist enshrouded the tops of the ragged black line of the forest that descended to the water's edge. The roar of the rapids and the dreariness of the inlet under low grey clouds gave the place a mood of unrelieved wildness. It was another connection I was able to make with the men of the Vancouver expedition, who spent many nights camped out along the shores of the Inland Sea, all of it then a wilderness of danger, harshness and fear.

I carried this thought with me the next day as I sailed up the last miles of the Inland Sea to Cape Caution, where I bade farewell to the Vancouver expedition. Lying off the cape, I again asked my question: Would I have wanted to be a member of the expedition, and if so, why? After following the expedition for more than a thousand miles, my answer to the first part of that question is an emphatic "yes."

The "why" I have already answered in my introduction earlier in this narrative. I am, I wrote, "a restless person ... a participant at the threshold of something that gives significance to the present moment and a passionate anticipation for the unknown future." Every day spent following Vancouver, every mile travelled, fulfilled those desires of my personality, that of a man who would like to have been an 18th-century maritime explorer, even if his role was limited to rowing a ship's boat through the Inland Sea.

XVIII.

My Invisible Crew

I WAS GIVEN THE ACCLAIM OF THE RETURNING VOYAGER WHEN I got back to *Kea*'s home port in Boston Harbor. That I had sailed the length of the Inland Sea *alone* was considered quite an accomplishment. True, I had sailed the length of that sea, not run aground nor damaged *Kea* in any way, but alone I was not, because of those writers, voyagers, inventors and scientists who sailed with me as my invisible crew.

I bought *Kea* in late life to become something of the man I had always wanted to be: a sailor-adventurer looking for what author Jonathan Raban, in his foreword to Miles Smeeton's book *Once Is Enough*, describes as the objective of sailing "order, purpose, social harmony and the sublimation of the self to a large and romantic ideal."

The man I had wanted to be lived in the literature of the sea, in the journals of maritime explorers and in the stories of men who made outstanding sea voyages. My heroes were those men of book and journal who inspired me to make my Inland Sea voyage and sailed with me as my invisible crew.

There were many. Joshua Slocum, of course, who made the first solo circumnavigation of the world in 1895–96 in his famous sloop, *Spray*. In his book *Sailing Alone Around the World*, he wrote: "Dangers there are, to be sure, on the sea as well as on the land, but the intelligence and skill God gives to man reduce these to a minimum ... To face the elements is, to be sure, no light matter when the sea is in its grandest mood. You must then know the sea and know that you know it, and not forget that it was made to be sailed over."

Harry Pidgeon was the farmer who became a sailor, built his yawl *Islander* on the mud flats of Los Angeles, then sailed it around the world in 1921. In his book, *Around the World Single-Handed,* he offered me a challenge that sometimes saw me through from one tiring day to another: "You can sail for one day, can't you [and] that's all it is — one day after another." Then there was the romantic Alain Gerbault, French tennis star and *bon vivant*, who made a six-year, 40,000-mile solo circumnavigation in *Firecrest* in 1923, wrecking his boat twice along the way.

First and foremost among the men I admired was H. W. "Bill" Tilman, world-famous English mountain and ocean explorer. Of all my heroes, Tilman is the man I would most have liked to sail with. We shared a penchant for a rather Spartan form of simplicity and a mutual taste for wooden boats, pipe smoke, rum and woollen clothes.

Tilman served in both world wars and in the period between the two he made significant climbs in the Himalayas. In his 50s, unable to continue high-elevation climbing, he turned to the sea and sailing with the purchase of the 50-year-old British pilot cutter

Mischief. In this boat, he made three year-long voyages to the South Atlantic that took him to the icefields of Tierra del Fuego and the remote and distant Kerguelen, Crozets and South Georgia islands.

Then, in a final orgy of sea adventures, he made 13 voyages to Greenland and Baffin Island, losing on those voyages both *Mischief* and its even more decrepit successor, the old pilot boat *Sea Breeze.* His last voyage at age 80 was aboard the converted tug *En Avant* that went down with all hands somewhere in the South Atlantic on its way to the Antarctic.

Bill Tilman, for me, more than earned the status of hero that today is too easily applied to men of lesser achievements. It is not because of his achievements that I revere him, but because of the man himself. He was stubborn, rash, sometime foolhardy, but always the romantic in pursuit of a distant mountain peak or a voyage to an icy sea in a personal effort to make a life in old age still worth living.

And throughout my cruise, I recalled long-distance voyager Eric Hiscock's definition of seamanship. "Seamanship," he wrote in *Cruising Under Sail,* "is an art that can always be improved upon, with something fresh to learn each time one goes afloat ... and a lifetime can be spent attempting to reach perfection."

Perfection I do not expect to achieve. But within the reach for perfection — whatever its expression — lies the art of living at its most rewarding level. For me, that art is expressed in sailing a boat in the winds, weather, tides and dangers of the Inland Sea.

And there are others I must credit as members of my invisible crew — not voyagers, but men of scientific and technical skills. For example, when I use my arm-powered winches to lift the mainsail or tighten the jib sheets, I am able to do so with minimum muscular effort because of a law of physics discovered by the Greek scientist Archimedes, 287 to 212 B.C. Remember him? He's the man who believed that if he had a place to stand on and a lever long enough, he could move the world. In understanding the principle of the lever, he was able to state the law of physics that says if distance increases, the effort of moving an object is lessened. Walk up a steep stairway and the effort is great; walk up the longer but less steep stairway and the effort decreases. The same principle applies to the halyard with which I lift the mainsail. The length of the halyard is twice the distance of the lifted sail so the effort to lift it is halved. With the winches I use to trim the mainsail and jib sheets, "distance" is gained on the rope to be pulled by the many revolutions I crank with the winch handle. The same principle applies to the block-and-tackle system I use to lift the dinghy aboard the boat.

The law discovered by another scientist, the 18th-century Swiss physicist Daniel Bernoulli, explains why *Kea* sails and, understanding why, I can sail it more efficiently. I look up the big, red, wind-filled belly of the mainsail and the clean curve of the jib and it looks like the boat is being "pushed" by that wind. Wrong, says Bernoulli's law. Instead of being pushed by the wind, the boat is continually moving forward into the low-pressure area in front of the sails. The Bernoulli principle states that the pressure of moving air decreases as its velocity increases (increase in velocity, decrease in pressure). The principle works this way: my sail — like the wing of a bird or an airplane — presents a curved surface to the wind. Air flowing around the longer, outside curve of the sail moves faster than the air flowing along the flat surface to produce a suction force (decreased air pressure) that pulls the boat forward. It's not too romantic to say that I am "sucked along" over the water, but that is how the boat sails.

Germany's Rudolph Diesel invented the diesel engine and to him I am indebted because on many windless days I used *Kea*'s small diesel engine. In his book *Diesel's Engine*, author Lyle Cummins writes that when the young Diesel was in polytechnic school, he was fascinated by a pneumatic tinder igniter. Looking like a simple bicycle pump, it demonstrated how heat generated by compression in the pump could ignite a piece of tinder in the end of the pump. Diesel never forgot this demonstration and he dedicated his life and fortune to incorporating the principle of that pump into an efficient power machine. He called it his "Black Mistress" because it cost him so much in time and money.

My 10-horsepower Yanmar engine was developed by the Japanese industrialist Magokichi Yamaoka, who saw his first diesel engine at an industrial fair in Leipzig, Germany, in 1932. Something of a visionary, as was Diesel himself, Yamaoka thought that a small diesel engine with fuel economy would suit the needs of the Japanese farmer. In 1933, he developed a very small, five-horse-power engine, believing that in oil-poor Japan, a drop of fuel was equal to a drop of blood.

A French chef, Nicolas Appert, who invented the canning process of food preservation in the early 19th century, is responsible for the choices I had for my dinners: tuna with noodles; tuna with rice; chicken with noodles; chicken with rice. To each, I can add a can of vegetables — peas, beans or corn — for unlimited variations. My canned dinners did become monotonous, but remembering the food choices of Vancouver's men — salt pork and beef — made them more palatable.

With these companions, then — my English, French and American sailing heroes, Greek and Swiss scientists, a German inventor and a French chef — I was able to sail behind the Vancouver expedition, eat well and keep *Kea* moving in wind or calm.

Now, tied to my home dock in Boston Harbor, Vancouver's voyage and the thousand-mile voyage I made to follow it is behind me. Shamelessly, I used that expedition as an excuse to lay claim to that Inland Sea as mine, as Vancouver claimed it for his king and country. My claim, however, is not by deed but by the love I formed for the area's dramatic sea-washed shores of rock, beach, forest and cliff and its more subtle elements: the silent cat's paw of the approaching wind, the root of a tree struggling to find sustenance in the crack of the glacier-scoured rock, the liquid rush of the tiny wave up the beach that heralds the incoming tide.

In a way, my voyage was a kind of concluding biography of how I have lived and what I have lived for; that previously described restless person, "who has always been on the move toward the edge of what he knows, with the desire to cross over that edge to something unknown."

In that voyage, I crossed over that edge and, having done so, I no longer have to pursue that goal. But still, a-sailing I will go, if only to the limited horizons of Peter Puget's sound. Short voyages these will be, more about *being* somewhere than *going* somewhere. No charts or compass will be required to find my way along courses set by whatever the direction of wind and tide may be. Each voyage will be a circumnavigation: outward bound to no particular destination and back again to a safe port. There will be time along the way to notice the changes in weather and sky, the fluctuating tide and the shorelines of summer green and winter brown as I sail familiar waters, discovering along the way the hidden secrets of exploration.

XIX.

Beyond Cape Caution

I DID NOT FOLLOW VANCOUVER BEYOND CAPE CAUTION, BUT TO complete the narrative of his expedition I include a brief description of his exploration beyond the cape.

From Cape Caution, the two ships sailed across Queen Charlotte Strait to an anchorage in Smith Inlet. For the next 10 days, boat expeditions working out from the anchored ships explored the fractured mainland coast in stormy weather and dangerous seas. These explorations carried the boat crews into Smith Inlet, Fitz Hugh Sound and Burke Channel (honouring the Right Honourable Edmund Burke). One entry by Vancouver describes the general conditions encountered in this section of the survey: " ... stupendous mountains, and nearly perpendicular, rocky cliffs, producing pine trees to a considerable height above the shores, and then nearly barren to their lofty summits, which were mostly covered with snow ... as desolate inhospitable a country as the most melancholy creature could be desirous of inhabiting. The eagle, crow, and raven that occasionally had borne us company in our lonely researches, visited not these dreary shores."

Another entry comments on the weather the boat crews experienced: "The weather, though clear at intervals for a short time, continuing very boisterous, filled our minds with much solicitude for the welfare of our friends in the boats ... who were greatly exposed not only to its inclemency, but to the violence of the sea, which, from an uninterrupted ocean, broke with great fury on the southern shores."

Puget's remarks, after nights sleeping in the boats with sails his only cover, concluded this 10-day survey: "We at length reached the Rendezvous & stood over to Safety Cove, most heartily tired of the Expedition by such a Series of bad Weather."

On August 19, the two ships sailed out of Smith Inlet, rounded Cape Scott and sailed down the coast to Nootka Sound to conclude the 1792 survey. There, Vancouver was greeted by Juan Francisco de la Bodega y Quadra, the Spanish governor of Nootka. Diplomatic conversations began that eventually led to the Nookta Treaty, which ceded the sound to England. During these negotiations, Vancouver wrote: "Sen' Quadra had very earnestly requested that I would name some port or island after us both, to commemorate our meeting and the very friendly intercourse that had taken place and subsisted between us. Conceiving no spot so proper for the denomination as the place where we had first met, which was nearly in the centre of a tract of land that had first been circumnavigated by us ... I named that country the island of Quadra and Vancouver."

And so the name of the island remained until the Hudson's Bay Company shortened it to "Vancouver Island."

Vancouver then sailed to Hawaii to refit his ships, but by May of 1793 he was back on the northwest coast to pick up the survey where it had ended the year before. The second-year survey examined over 700 miles of the continental edge in 23 days, all by oar and sail in the ship's boats. Vancouver then returned to Hawaii for a winter layover. For his third survey year, he decided to start at the known location of Cook Inlet, which he had visited previously on Captain James Cook's last voyage. After all the other inlets and sounds had ended in mountain ranges, this broad inlet was the last hope for the water passage across North America. He entered the inlet in May of 1794 after a brutally cold voyage through the Gulf of Alaska. Huge tides, rocks and floating ice were the added hazards of the boat expeditions as they worked up to the end of the inlet.

Prince William Sound, with its towering glacier walls, was surveyed, followed by Cross Sound, Glacier Bay, Lynn Canal and Chatham Strait. The ships were worn out, the men tired and Vancouver's health confined him to his cabin. Calling an end to the survey, the two ships left the coast in November, headed south through the Pacific, rounded Cape Horn, sailed up the Atlantic and stopped at St. Helena. There, the *Discovery* and the *Chatham* parted, the latter for Brazil to join a convoy for a safe passage back to England (England and France at this time were at war). In September of 1795, the *Discovery* anchored in Shannon, Ireland, to end Vancouver's four-year voyage to the Pacific coast.

For all those miles, through all those dangers, cold and rain, only six men in a crew of over 200 had died. Vancouver, however, was a very sick man. Racing death, he was unable to complete his journal before he died in May of 1798. His brother John completed the book.

Vancouver's legacy is what he found and what he did not find (that Northwest Passage), and the survey he made of the northwest coast, which gave to that coast a British identity and claim.

His modest headstone in the churchyard in Petersham, England, bears the simple inscription "Captain George Vancouver/Died in the Year 1778/Age 40." But far to the west, across the oceans he crossed, stand an island and a city that bear his name. And in Victoria — just across from the city of Vancouver — his statue stands at the provincial legislature, looking out toward the waters he sailed.

AFTERWORD:

Place Names in History

Place names are a very important form of communication. By a name, a place is given specific identity and in that name is a reflection of native cultures, exploration and settlement. A name on a map or chart is a place to go to or, if the journey cannot be made, a place to imagine and dream about.

Names bestowed across the charts of the Inland Sea are a mix of myth, religion, topographical descriptions, personal vanities, pioneer settlers, national leaders, heroes, patrons and superiors.

But what is so apparent in the majority of these names is that the history of the Inland Sea is predominantly a maritime history with the names of maritime explorers, ships, ship captains and admirals the legacy of that history. Out of the Spanish, English and American explorations of the late 18th and early 19th century emerge those names. Long, difficult and hazardous were those voyages along the coasts of these northern waters, and with each mile charted and named, an incremental addition was made to a part of the world previously unknown. A name left behind on these voyages was a place fixed in location that could be the objective of other journeys by sea or land.

To a large extent, the history of naming a place was a self-appointed task. Those who felt they were "first" at a place assumed the right to name it. With so many assuming that right — whether Aboriginal, explorer, pioneer or settler — confusion in coastal place names was inevitable and troublesome for the map makers (to say nothing of the post offices). In 1847, Captain Henry Kellet of the British Admiralty published a series of internationally accepted charts that established the present place names we find on the charts today.

I have, below, included just a few of the names of major seascape places passed on my voyage around the Inland Sea. For a more complete listing of Washington historical names, refer to James W. Phillips' *Washington State Place Names*, published by the University of Washington Press. Captain John Walbran's *British Columbia Coast Names*, published by J. J. Douglas Ltd., Vancouver, is an excellent source for B.C. names.

Captain Walbran's book is also a very interesting narrative of British Columbia history. His research was gathered during his years as commander of the Canadian government steamship *Quadra*. As he travelled the coast doing survey work, he sought out first-hand surviving accounts of coastal history. In addition to giving the history of a name, he writes at great length with the kind of anecdotal information that brings this history to life. For example, I quote one of the entries discussed in the introduction to his book, the name history of Marchant Rock: "Marchant rock, off Otter passage, Hecate strait. After George Marchant, an old seafaring resident of this coast. The *Beaver's* [his ship] men, during the breakfast one fine morning in July, 1869, were resting on the rocks facing the waters of Hecate strait, when a breaker far seaward, persistently appearing in the same place, caught Marchant's eye ... the breaker was found to mark a dangerous off-lying rock, which was located and named after the discoverer, Marchant Rock."

I list below a few of the name places passed during my cruise.

WASHINGTON SEASCAPE NAMES

Admiralty Inlet: This strait connecting the Strait of Juan de Fuca with Puget Sound was named by Vancouver to honour the Board of Admiralty, which was in charge of Britain's naval affairs.

Agate Passage: This short passage at the northern tip of Bainbridge Island, connecting Port Madison with Port Orchard, was named for Alfred Agate, artist on the U.S. Navy's exploration expedition of 1838–42 commanded by Charles Wilkes.

Alki Point: The founders of the future city of Seattle, 12 adults and 12 children, landed on this southern point of Elliott Bay in 1851. Because the community was slow to grow, they adopted the Chinook word *alki*, which, roughly translated, meant the slow-time concept of "by and by."

Anacortes: A Spanish name given to this city by land developer Amos Bowman to honour not a Spaniard, but his wife, Anna Curtis.

Anderson Island: Alexander Anderson was the Hudson's Bay Company's chief trader at Fort Nisqually in the 1840s.

Bainbridge Island: It was Wilkes' habit to give names to places that honoured U.S. naval heroes. William Bainbridge had distinguished himself in the War of 1812 as captain of the ship *Constitution* (Old Ironsides).

Bellingham (Bay and City): Joseph Whidbey surveyed this bay in 1792, and Vancouver named it after Sir William Bellingham, keeper of the stores for the British navy.

Birch Bay: Vancouver, noting the many black birches along the shoreline of this bay, so named it.

Blakely Island: Wilkes named this island in the San Juans in honour of Johnston Blakely, commander of the U.S. Navy ship *Wasp* during the War of 1812.

Boundary Bay: So named because the boundary between the United States and Canada crosses this bay.

Budd Inlet: This inlet at the southern end of Puget Sound carries the name of Thomas Budd, an officer of the Wilkes expedition.

Cape Flattery: When James Cook was off this cape (which forms the northwest corner of Washington state) in 1778, he reported what "appeared to be a small opening that flattered us with hopes of finding a harbor there." The "small opening" observed by Cook was the Strait of Juan de Fuca.

Carr Inlet: Wilkes named this passage between Fox and McNeil islands for Lieutenant Overton Carr, a member of his expedition.

Cattle Point: This southern tip of San Juan Island was used by the Hudson's Bay Company as a site for loading and unloading cattle.

Commencement Bay: It was from this bay fronting the city of Tacoma that the Wilkes survey of lower Puget Sound began in May 1841.

Cypress Island: A botanical mistake by Vancouver, who thought the native pines of this island were cypress trees.

Dana Passage: This passage at the southern tip of Hartstene Island was named for James Dana, geologist with the Wilkes expedition.

Deception Pass: Joseph Whidbey did not see this narrow water passage on his exploration of Skagit Bay. Later, when the passage was observed, Vancouver gave it this name.

Doebay: Named (Doe Bay) because of the many deer on Orcas Island.

Ediz Hook: The name of this sandspit that forms the harbour of Port Angeles was derived from an Aboriginal word meaning a "good place."

Elliott Bay: Named for one of the three Elliotts with the Wilkes expedition, but the record is not clear as to which one of the three was honoured by the naming of this bay that fronts Seattle.

Foulweather Bluff: The name of this bluff at the eastern entrance to Hood Canal describes the weather experienced by Vancouver when he and his men camped there in May 1792. He wrote: "This promontory is not ill named, for we had scarcely landed, when a heavy rain commenced, which continuing the rest of the day, obliged us to remain stationary."

Friday Harbour: San Juan Island's largest town was named for "Friday," a Hawaiian employed by the Hudson's Bay Company to tend the company's island flock of sheep.

Gig Harbour: This small harbour was just deep enough to be entered by a ship's boat called a "gig," sent by Wilkes to survey the bay.

Haro Strait: This strait between San Juan Island and Vancouver Island was named for the Spanish explorer Lopez Gonzales de Haro. The U.S.–Canada border passes through Haro Strait.

Hood Canal: This waterway and Oregon's highest mountain were both named by Vancouver in honour of Samuel Hood, vice-admiral of the *Blue*, who signed the instructions for Vancouver's expedition. Hood was a member of a famous English naval family, and his distinguished career included commands in England's wars with France and during the American Revolution.

Lopez Island: Named for the Spanish maritime explorer Lopez Gonzales de Haro (also Haro Strait).

McNeil Island: William Henry McNeil was captain of the Hudson's Bay Company steamer *Beaver*, the first steam vessel on the coast. It was built in England, sailed around Cape Horn, and arrived at the Columbia River in 1836.

Marrowstone Island: Named by Vancouver, who wrote, "The high steep cliff, forming the point of land we were now upon, seemed to be principally composed ... [of] a rich species of the marrow stone, from whence it obtained the name of Marrow-Stone Point."

Mercer Island: Thomas Mercer was the captain of a wagon train that arrived in Seattle in 1853.

Mukilteo: The word is a variation of an Aboriginal name that means a good camping area.

Mutiny Bay: There should be a story behind the name of this small bay on the southwest shore of Whidbey Island, but it was named by the U.S. Coast Survey in 1855 without explanation.

Orcas Island: The full name of Spain's viceroy in Mexico in the 1790s was Juan Vincente de Guemes Pacheco de Padilla Horcacitas y Aguayo, Count of Revilla Gigedo. Fortunately, when this island was given his name, the "Horcacitas" was shortened to Orcas.

Point No Point: Less a point than it had appeared from a distance, this promontory projecting into Admiralty Inlet was given this descriptive name by Wilkes.

Point Partridge: Vancouver gives no explanation for the naming of this point on the southwest shore of Whidbey Island.

Port Angeles: First named Porto de Nuestra Senora de los Angeles ("Port of Our Lady of the Angels") by the Spanish captain Francisco Eliza in 1791, Vancouver shortened it to its present name.

Port Townsend: Named by Vancouver for the Marquis of Townshend, with the "h" dropped. After British General James Wolfe fell in the fight against the French at Quebec (1759), Townshend assumed command of the victorious British army.

Possession Sound: Named by Vancouver when, on June 4, 1792, he claimed for King George III all the waters and surrounding shores of Puget Sound, the Strait of Juan de Fuca and the Strait of Georgia.

Puget Sound: Explored in May 1792 by Lieutenant Peter Puget. Wrote Vancouver, "To commemorate Mr. Puget's exertions, the southern extremity of it I named Puget's Sound." Vancouver was referring to the southern end of the sound, but in time common usage referred to the entire sound by that name, but without the apostrophe.

San Juan Islands: The island group was named Isla y Archipelago de San Juan by de Haro in 1791 to honour the viceroy of Mexico (also Orcas Island).

Strait of Georgia: Named by Vancouver to honour King George III of England.

Strait of Juan de Fuca: Named for the Greek pilot Apostolos Valerianos, who, sailing for Spain with the name Juan de Fuca, claimed to have discovered this large strait on a voyage along the northwest coast in 1592. His claim — accepted during the early years of northwest coastal exploration — was honoured by Captain Charles Barkley, a British trader who named the strait.

Sucia Island: *Sucia* is a Spanish word meaning "dirty" but in a nautical sense, as Francisco Eliza used it to refer to the "foul" rocks and reefs around this island.

Useless Bay: Both Natives and Wilkes thought this shallow bay at the southern end of Whidbey Island worthless: *cultus*, meaning "bad" in the Aboriginal language, "useless" in English.

Vashon Island: Vancouver named this island in honour of Vice-Admiral James Vashon, a distinguished British naval officer who participated in sea battles of the American Revolution and the wars between England and France.

Wasp Island: Wilkes honoured Captain Jacob Jones of the American navy by naming this island after his ship, *Wasp*. Nearby Jones Island honours Jones himself.

Whidbey Island: Joseph Whidbey was sailing master aboard Vancouver's ship *Discovery*. Whidbey surveyed and charted this island in June 1792, and for his efforts, Vancouver gave his name to the island.

BRITISH COLUMBIA SEASCAPE NAMES

Active Pass: The channel running between Mayne and Galiano islands carries the name of the U.S. surveying ship *Active*, a wooden paddlewheel steamer.

Agamemnon Channel: This channel along the eastern shore of Nelson Island carries the name of the first line-of-battle ship to be commanded by England's great admiral Horatio Nelson.

Anvil Island: So named by Vancouver because this island in Howe Sound resembles an anvil.

Arran Rapids: Admiralty surveyors named this rapid at the northern end of Stuart Island for the Island of Arran in Scotland.

Ballenas Islands: "Islands of the Whales" are named after the numerous whales observed here by Lieutenant Francisco Eliza.

Brotchie Ledge: This reef just outside the entrance to Victoria's harbour carries the name of Captain William Brotchie, whose ship, *Albion*, struck the rock in 1849.

Broughton Island: Vancouver honoured Lieutenant William Broughton, commander of the escort vessel *Chatham*, by giving his name to this island group after Broughton's important exploration of the archipelago.

Burrard Inlet: The inlet that forms the city of Vancouver's harbour was named by Vancouver for his friend, Sir Henry Burrard, who had distinguished himself in the Napoleonic wars.

Bute Inlet: John Stuart, third Earl of Bute, was a prominent politician during the reign of King George III.

Cadboro Bay: This bay to the east of Victoria carries the name of the Hudson's Bay Company brigantine *Cadboro*, the first vessel to anchor in the bay in 1827. The ship was the first vessel to enter the Fraser River.

Cape Cockburn: Admiral Sir George Cockburn saw service in the English–French wars under Lord Nelson. During the War of 1812, Cockburn commanded the joint naval and military force that captured Washington, D.C.

Cape Mudge: Zachary Mudge, first lieutenant of *Discovery*, climbed a hill and first noted the inlet (Discovery Passage) that allowed the Vancouver expedition to sail north from the Strait of Georgia to Queen Charlotte Strait. Vancouver named this cape at the southern end of Quadra Island for him.

Chatham Point: The *Chatham* was the escort vessel that accompanied Vancouver on his 1792 survey of the Inland Sea. It, in turn, was named for the Earl of Chatham, First Lord of the Admiralty, by Vancouver.

Chemainus: The city was founded where, for thousands of years, the Chemainus First Nations lived.

Cortes Island: Cortes Island and Hernando Island to the south were named by Galiano and Valdés after Hernando Cortes, the Spanish conqueror of Mexico.

Cowichan Bay: Named for one of the bands of the Cowichan First Nations that lived along the shores of this bay.

Cracroft Islands: These two islands in Johnstone Strait are named for Sophia Cracroft, niece of the English explorer Sir John Franklin, who was lost with all his men in the fatal Arctic expeditions of the *Erebus* and *Terror*.

D'Arcy Island: Once a Chinese leper colony, this island in Haro Strait is now a provincial park. It carries the name of Lieutenant D'Arcy Denny, who commanded the gunboat *Forward* in B.C. waters in the 1860s.

Desolation Sound: To Vancouver, Desolation Sound was a gloomy place where "an awful silence pervaded the gloomy forests, whilst animated nature seemed to have deserted the neighboring country."

Dodd Narrows: Formerly called Nanaimo Rapids, this narrow tide-running channel was named for Captain Charles Dodd, commander of the Hudson's Bay Company steamboat *Beaver*.

Eden Island: Vice-Admiral Charles Eden, one of the Lords of the Admiralty, commanded HMS *London* during the English–Russian war of 1854–55.

Fife Sound: This channel running south of Broughton Island was named by Vancouver for James Duff, second Earl of Fife. During a food famine in Scotland in 1782, he imported grain from England to feed the poor.

Fraser River: Simon Fraser was a partner in the fur-trading North West Company. He led an exploration party down the Fraser in 1808, believing before he reached its mouth that it was the Columbia River.

Galiano Island: Dionisio Alcalá Galiano commanded the Spanish ship *Sutil* and was in charge of the Spanish 1792 exploration of the straits of Juan de Fuca, Georgia and Queen Charlotte. Vancouver encountered this expedition on his circumnavigation of Vancouver Island, and the two expeditions proceeded in cooperation with each other as they continued their surveys of the coast.

Ganges: This town on Saltspring Island carries the name of HMS *Ganges*, the last sailing ship of the line built for the British navy. The ship was on active duty at the Esquimalt naval station from 1857 to 1860. Built of teak in India, the ship was 108 years old before being scrapped in 1929.

Point Grey: Named by Vancouver for Captain George Grey, a distinguished English officer who saw action in numerous battles in the English–French wars.

Helmcken Island: John Sebastian Helmcken was a medical officer for the Hudson's Bay Company in Victoria from 1850 to 1886.

Hernando Island: This island in the northern end of the Strait of Georgia takes the name of Hernando Cortes, conqueror of Mexico.

Homfray Channel: This channel leading out of Desolation Sound carries the name of civil engineer Robert Homfray, who trained under Isambard Brunel, the eminent engineer who designed and built the huge transatlantic steamship *Great Eastern*.

Hornby Island: Rear-Admiral Phipps Hornby served as a junior officer with Nelson aboard HMS *Victory*.

Howe Sound: A captain in the Royal Navy at 21, the Right Honourable Earl of Howe was one of England's most illustrious naval officers.

Jervis Inlet: Named by Vancouver for Rear-Admiral John Jervis, who entered the Royal Navy as an able seaman and became the celebrated Earl St. Vincent after his victory in 1797 over a superior Spanish fleet.

Johnstone Strait: James Johnstone was master of Vancouver's escort vessel, *Chatham*. It was his discovery of this strait that allowed the expedition to make the first circumnavigation of Vancouver Island.

Kingcome Inlet: In a coastal survey in 1865, this inlet was named for Rear-Admiral John Kingcome, who was commander in chief of the B.C. station in 1863–64.

Knight Inlet: During the American Revolution, Second Lieutenant John Knight, RN, was taken prisoner, and his fellow prisoner was a young midshipman by the name of William Broughton. Broughton, later commander of Vancouver's escort ship *Chatham*, explored the inlet and named it in remembrance of his fellow prisoner.

Ladysmith: James Dunsmuir, lieutenant-governor of British Columbia, celebrated the relief of Ladysmith, South Africa, during the Boer War by the naming of this Vancouver Island town. The African city was named for Lady Smith, a member of Spanish nobility and a lineal descendant of Ponce de Leon.

Loughborough Inlet: Named by Vancouver for Alexander Wedderburn, first Lord Loughborough, who in 1793 was appointed Lord High Chancellor of England.

Malaspina Strait: Alexandro Malaspina was an Italian who served in Spain's navy. Between 1789 and 1794, Malaspina commanded an around-the-world Spanish expedition of exploration and science.

Marina Island: This Sutil Channel island is named for Hernando Cortes' mistress, the famous Marina, who also served Cortes as an interpreter during his conquest of Mexico.

Mayne Island: One of the Gulf Islands, Mayne was named for Lieutenant Richard Mayne, RN, who served aboard the survey vessel *Plumper* from 1857 to 1860.

Menzies Bay: Archibald Menzies served as botanist on the Vancouver expedition.

Moresby Island: This island in Haro Strait carries the name of Rear-Admiral Fairfax Moresby, active during the 1820s in suppressing the African slave trade.

Nanaimo: The city name is derived from the Aboriginal name for the five tribes that banded together in this area under the name "Sne-ny-mo" (Snuneymuxw).

Nelson Island: This island in Malaspina Strait was named for Admiral Horatio Nelson, England's great naval hero.

Newcastle Island: This island off Nanaimo was named for the old coal city of Newcastle upon Tyne, Northumberland.

Pender Islands (North and South): These Gulf Islands bear the name of Daniel Pender, second master of the survey vessel *Plumper*. After becoming master of the steamer *Beaver*, Pender continued his hydrographic survey here to its conclusion in 1870.

Portland Island: Now Princess Margaret Marine Park, Portland Island in Haro Strait was named after HMS *Portland*, flagship of Rear Admiral Fairfax Moresby, who commanded the Pacific station, 1850–53.

Prevost Island: Captain James Prevost, RN, served on the Pacific station in 1850. Upon his return to England, he was appointed a commissioner for settling the San Juan Island border dispute.

Pylades Channel: HMS *Pylades*, a steam-powered corvette, served on the Pacific station in 1859–61 and again in 1868. Among the ship's officers in 1868 was a son of Charles Dickens.

Quadra Island: The Geographic Board of Canada in 1903 named this island to honour Juan Francisco de la Bodega y Quadra, one-time Spanish governor at Nootka.

Rebecca Spit: Rebecca Spit on Quadra Island is named for the trading schooner *Rebecca,* one of the small ships active in coastal trade in the 1860s.

Saltspring Island: So named by officers of the Hudson's Bay Company because of salty springs found on the island.

Sansum Narrows: Arthur Sansum served aboard HMS *Thetis,* active on the Pacific station, 1851–53. Sansum Narrows runs between Saltspring and Vancouver islands.

Saturna Island: This Gulf Island carries the name of the Spanish naval schooner, *Santa Saturnina,* commanded by Jose Maria Narvaez. He named the island during his 1791 exploration of the Strait of Georgia.

Scotch Fir Point: On this prominent point at the northern entrance to Jervis Inlet, Vancouver noted trees that to him resembled Scotch firs.

Seymour Narrows: Sir George Francis Seymour was in command of the Pacific station, 1844–48. After a long and active career in the Royal Navy, he retired with the rank of admiral in 1866.

Sonora Island: Named for the Spanish schooner *Sonora,* a small, 36-foot vessel commanded by Quadra in which he explored along the northwest coast in 1775.

Texada Island: Jose Narvaez, in command of the Spanish exploring vessel *Santa Saturnina,* named this large island in 1791.

Thormanby Islands: The racehorse Thormanby was the winner of the Derby in 1860.

Toba Inlet: Spanish explorers found here a table (*tabla*) of planks with Native carvings on them. An engraving error on the chart drawn of the area changed "Tabla" to "Toba" and so the name has remained.

Trincomali Channel: Named for HMS *Trincomali*, a 24-gun frigate that saw duty on the Pacific station from 1852 to 1856.

Yuculta Rapids: These rapids carry the name of an Aboriginal tribe that lived in the area.

Bibliography

Armstrong, Dr. John. *Vancouver Geology*. Vancouver, B.C.: Geological Association of Canada, 1990.

Beaglehole, J.C. *The Journals of Captain Cook and his Voyages of Discovery*. Cambridge and London, U.K.: The Hakluyt Society, 1955–1974.

Berry, Don. *To Build a Ship*. New York, N.Y.: Viking Press, 1963.

Barman, Jean. *A History of British Columbia*. Toronto, Ont.: University of Toronto Press, 1991.

Bascom, Willard. *Waves and Beaches: The Dynamics of the Ocean Surface*. Garden City, N.Y.: Doubleday & Company, 1964.

Beals, Herbert. *The Last Temperate Coast, Maritime Exploration of Northwest America, 1542–1794*. Portland, Ore.: Oregon Historical Society, 1990.

Canadian Hydrographic Service. *Sailing Directions, British Columbia Coast (South Portion)*. Volume l. Sidney, B.C.: Department of Fisheries and Oceans, 1990.

Chemainus Festival of Murals Society. *The Chemainus Murals*. Chemainus, B.C.: Chemainus Murals Society, 1993.

Cummings, Lyle. *Diesel's Engine*. Wilsonville, Ore.: Carnot Press, 1993.

Dening, Greg. *Mr. Bligh's Bad Language*. New York, N.Y.: Cambridge University Press, 1992.

Drucker, Philip. *Indians of the Northwest Coast*. Garden City, N.Y.: The Natural History Press, 1955.

Fisher, Robin and Hugh Johnston. *From Maps to Metaphors: The Pacific World of George Vancouver*. Vancouver, B.C.: University of British Columbia Press, 1993.

Fisher, Robin. *Vancouver's Voyage, Charting the Northwest Coast, 1791–1795*. Vancouver, B.C.: Douglas & McIntyre, 1992.

Gough, Barry M. *Distant Dominion, Britain and the Northwest Coast of North America, 1579–1809*. Vancouver, B.C.: University of British Columbia Press, 1980.

Gulf Islands Branch, BC Historical Association. *A Gulf Islands Patchwork*. Pender Island, B.C.: 1961.

Hiscock, Eric. *Cruising Under Sail*. Camden, Maine: International Marine Publishing Company, 1996.

Kemp, Peter. *The Oxford Companion to Ships and the Sea*. Oxford, U.K.: Oxford University Press, 1993.

Kennedy, Liv. *Coastal Villages*. Madeira Park, B.C.: Harbour Publishing, 1991.

Lamb, W. Kaye. *George Vancouver: A Voyage of Discovery to the North Pacific Ocean*. London, U.K.: The Hakluyt Society, 1984.

Lillard, Charles. *Seven Shillings a Year: The History of Vancouver Island*. Ganges, B.C.: Horsdal & Schubart Publishers Ltd., 1986.

Lopez, Barry. *Arctic Dreams*. New York, N.Y.: Scribner's, 1986.

McCurdy, James G. *By Juan de Fuca's Strait*. Portland, Ore.: Metropolitan Press, 1937.

Meany, Edmond S. *Vancouver's Discovery of Puget Sound*. Portland, Ore.: Binfords & Mort, 1957.

Morgan, Murray and Rosa. *South on the Sound*. Woodland Hills, Calif.: Windsor Publications, Inc., 1984.

Murray, Peter. *Homesteads and Snug Harbours: The Gulf Islands*. Ganges, B.C.: Horsdal & Schubart Publishers Ltd., 1991.

Nelson, Sharlene P. and Ted. *Washington Lighthouses*. Friday Harbor, Wash.: Umbrella Books, 1990.

Nicholson, George. *Vancouver Island's West Coast*. Victoria, B.C.: George Nicholson, 1965.

Pacific Northwest Quarterly. Volume 33. Seattle, Wash.: University of Washington Press, April 1934.

Phillips, James W. *Washington State Place Names*. Seattle, Wash.: University of Washington Press, 1990.

Pidgeon, Harry. *Around the World Single-Handed*. New York, N.Y.: John de Graff, Inc., 1955.

Poe, Edgar Allan. *Complete Works*. New York, N.Y.: Lamb Publishing Co., 1902.

Rodger, N.A.M. *The Wooden World: An Anatomy of the Georgian Navy*. Annapolis, Maryland: Naval Institute Press, 1986.

Slocum, Joshua. *Sailing Alone Around the World*. New York, N.Y.: Dover Publications, 1956.

Smeeton, Miles (with introduction by Jonathan Raban). *Once is Enough*. Camden, Maine: International Marine Publishing Company, 2001.

Swan, James. *The Northwest Coast*. Seattle, Wash.: University of Washington Press, 1977.

Tanod, Lynn and Chris Jaksa. *Guiding Lights: British Columbia's Lighthouses and their Keepers*. Madeira Park, B.C.: Harbour Publishing, 1998.

Thomson, Richard. *Oceanography of the British Columbia Coast*. Ottawa, Ont.: Department of Fisheries and Oceans, 1981.

U.S. Department of Commerce, National Oceanic and Atmospheric Administration. *United States Coast Pilot, Pacific Coast: California, Oregon, Washington and Hawaii*. Washington, D.C., 1994.

Walbran, John T. *British Columbia Coast Names*. Vancouver, B.C.: J.J. Douglas, 1971.

Woodcock, George. *British Columbia: A History of the Province*. Vancouver, B.C.: Douglas & McIntyre, 1990.

The late Sam McKinney was a former research associate at the Vancouver Maritime Museum, and had been a journalist, teacher of Outward Bound programs and builder of small boats. He is the author of *Bligh! The Whole Story of the Mutiny Aboard HMS Bounty*; *Reach of Tide, Ring of History*; and *Sailing Uphill: An Unconventional Life on the Water*.